THE SELF-HELP WAY
TO TREAT COLITIS
AND OTHER IBS
DISORDERS

THE SELF-HELP WAY TO TREAT COLITIS AND OTHER IBS DISORDERS

De Lamar Gibbons, M.D.

Keats Publishing, Inc. New Canaan, Connecticut

The Self-Help Way to Treat Colitis and Other IBS Disorders is not intended as medical advice. Its intent is solely informational and educational. Please consult a health professional should the need for one be indicated.

THE SELF-HELP WAY TO TREAT COLITIS
AND OTHER IBS DISORDERS

Copyright © 1992 by De Lamar Gibbons, M.D.

Library of Congress Cataloging in Publication Data

Gibbons, De Lamar.
    The self-help way to treat colitis and other IBS disorders / De Lamar Gibbons.
        p.   cm.
    Includes bibliographical references.
    ISBN 0-87983-546-X
    1. Irritable colon—Diet therapy.   I. Title.
RC862.I77G53   1992
616.3'42—dc20   92-3477
                                              CIP

Printed in the United States of America

Keats Publishing, Inc.
27 Pine Street (Box 876)
New Canaan, Connecticut 06840-0876

Contents

Preface

There is an old adage that says, "If you want the very best medical care, find a doctor who has the same ailment as you." In *The Self-Help Way to Treat Colitis and Other IBS Disorders*, I share my personal experience in dealing with this problem, and the observations gleaned in treating many patients with these maladies. The approach taken in the understanding and treatment recommended here is primarily from a chemical point of view. I believe that many health problems—including irritable bowel disease—are best treated when their chemical considerations are taken into account.

The observation that half of the people in the country are diet experts is probably an underestimation. There are so many "authorities" that people in the general public are unable to tell where to turn for sound advice. While there are many authorities, few can claim degrees in both chemistry and medicine to provide a scientific basis for their advice. I am a graduate of Utah State University and George Washington University School of Medicine.

For three years, I was research director for *The Sat-*

urday Evening Post. In this capacity, I surveyed more than 2,500 people with irritable bowel disease and shared with them this formula for the rational dietary management of these ailments: the Colitis Club Diet. Of the first thousand people returning surveys, nearly all (90.4 percent) reported great benefit from the diet. More than 25,000 more wrote in for the diet and hundreds sent letters of appreciation for freeing them from their "water closet imprisonment."

This book expands the admittedly brief information provided in the research diet. Its treatment regimen is aimed primarily at educating irritable bowel disease victims so they may regain control of their bodies and return their digestive systems to normal function. I hope hereby to spare many of my readers the horrible ravages of inflammation of the intestines.

Parts of this book are redundant. I make no apology. Important concepts are repeated for emphasis and clarity. The book is not intended as a replacement for your personal physician, but only as a supplement to his or her care. The suggestions I make will prove very helpful for the majority of irritable bowel disease patients, but guarantees are not implied and no responsibility for failure to improve is assumed.

You will not learn about colitis in after-dinner conversations. It is not a popular dinner or talk show topic. Neither is adequate information available to the general public on this unmentionable subject. This book addresses this information vacuum and provides new insights resulting from recent advances in the understanding and management of these diseases.

Some new developments are not generally known by

physicians. Probably the newest of these is the role *fructose* plays in the causation of bowel irritation. Fructose is the sugar found in sweet fruits and, in recent years, has been made synthetically from corn. Called "corn sweetener," it is an artificial honey. This sugar is twice as sweet as cane sugar and is less expensive to produce. It has been stealthfully substituted for cane and beet sugars in our diets. It replaces these sugars in waffle syrup, ice cream, candy, soda pop and numerous other foods.

For most people, it is a good and wholesome food. Most are able to convert it into glucose and burn it for energy. But for those with irritable bowel disease, it is the major irritating factor. Fructose intolerance is an inherited metabolic inability to digest this sugar due to the absence of an enzyme in the digestive system. The intake of excessive amounts of it may induce serious bowel irritation, manifested by voluminous intestinal gas production, cramping, diarrhea and rectal itching. The treatment is to reduce fructose in the diet.

A similar intolerance to lactose is another major source of bowel irritation. Lactose is the sugar naturally occurring in milk. Persons with irritable bowel disease should avoid milk until it can be established that the individual is not lactose intolerant. The conversion of lactose to glucose requires the enzyme lactase, that many lack. When lactose is not converted and absorbed, colonic bacteria ferment it to produce intestinal gas, bloating, abdominal pain, diarrhea and irritation of the lining of the intestine.

You may not need to avoid all of the items in each category listed on the diets provided in this book. These are only guidelines directing you to the foods most likely to cause irritation of the bowel. Some individuals will find they tolerate fructose and not lactose. Others will find the opposite applies to them. Many will find they are bothered by both sugars. However, as a rule, individuals with active irritable bowel disease should avoid eating large amounts of *any* sugars.

It should be noted that all people are intolerant of large amounts of sorbitol and mannitol. These are *alcohol sugars* that are not digested by any of us and are thus calorie-free. Taken in sufficient amounts, however, they will cause irritable bowel disease in all people. They provoke trouble because they ferment in the colon. These sweeteners are found in so-called sugar-free candy, breath mints, chewing gum, toothpaste and in some processed meats.

Celiac sprue is another hereditary problem. It can appear early or late in life as another cause of devastating bowel problems. It is due to intolerance to the protein *gluten* found in wheat, rye, barley and oats. This protein irritates the lining of the bowel resulting in chronic diarrhea. Consequently, there is a failure to digest and absorb vitamins, proteins and fats from the diet. This malabsorption is important because it leads to malnutrition. With gluten intolerance, there is usually lactose and/or fructose intolerance.

Each year, about 23,000 Americans have their colons removed and colostomy openings made in their abdominal walls because of the damage done to these organs by colitis and related conditions. No one should have such surgery without first determining whether or not they are intolerant of these everyday foods. Many will respond to following the dietary treatment outlined here and surgery will be unnecessary when the offending food elements are eliminated.

De Lamar Gibbons, M.D.

Introduction

Had Moses's followers been afflicted with irritable
bowel disease, the land "flowing with milk and honey"
would have held little attraction for them.

Irritable bowel syndrome (IBS) is the most common of
all the chronic disorders. It is estimated that 10 to 20
percent of the adult population have it. There is good
reason to believe a far greater number have mild forms
of the affliction, but attach little significance to their
symptoms (or perhaps they are too embarrassed to bring
them to the attention of their doctors).

The number of people who have mild symptoms of
irritable bowel disease, i.e., excessive intestinal gas formation; frequent bouts of diarrhea, abdominal cramps,
rectal itching; "pencil" or "ribbon" shaped stools; or
blood or mucus in the stool, is legion. Of those who seek
medical help, most are given antispasmodic drugs which
do not treat the source of the problem but are, like aspi-
rin, given for symptomatic relief only.

For those treated in this manner, the problem goes
on interminably. The treatment suggested in this book

xiii

is aimed at *eliminating the causes* of irritable bowel disease, not relying on cortisone or the chemotherapeutic agents used in treating cancer. Most irritable bowel disease can be controlled by diet—but you must know the principles involved. The treatment outlined in this book is based upon the application of a little basic chemistry.

Proper treatment of these conditions is important even though the symptoms may be mild, because continued irritation leads to more serious ulceration of the bowel, to malnutrition, anemia, weakness, diverticulosis, kidney stones, gallstones, arthritis and greatly increases one's chances for developing cancer of the colon.

Until now, the cause of these disorders has been a mystery and the treatment only palliative—and sometimes barbaric. Not uncommonly, a colectomy—the surgical removal of the colon and the establishment of a colostomy, an opening in the abdominal wall for fecal waste—was required to help unfortunate victims. More than 23,000 people suffer this operation annually. It is my hope that the number of individuals requiring colostomies in the future will be greatly reduced by the guidelines of this book.

The Colitis Club research diet was first offered to the readers of *The Saturday Evening Post* troubled with irritable bowel symptoms. Soon after the diet was offered, the mail began pouring in. More than 25,000 people requested it. Included with the diets were survey forms to be filled out by the individuals after they had tried the diet for a month. The respondents to the survey overwhelmingly reported improvement in their condition while following the diet guidelines. Many reported that prior to trying the research diet, they had been unable to leave their homes because of chronic diarrhea, or that medications had not given them satisfactory relief. The diet is now helping many with a wide variety of intestinal disorders, including ulcerative colitis, Crohn's disease or regional enteritis, spastic colon, irritable bowel syndrome and other undiagnosed bowel problems.

Hundreds of letters were received from grateful recipients thanking us for the help the diet had been to them. Typical letters read:

"Diet has brought about much improvement, I am apparently fructose intolerant."

"Bloated painful feeling on right side of abdomen has been eliminated. Also diarrhea is replaced by normal stools."

"I am beginning to have enough confidence to go out in public again after 15 years of misery. Thank you."

"I am very grateful I came across a copy of your magazine with the article about the diet. Before I tried it, I ate large quantities of fruit and I was in great pain with my bowels, I had malnutrition, anemia, weakness, and diverticulosis."

"I can never thank you enough! After having gone through x-rays twice in 8 years (finding nothing), and with no help from my doctors, I now have no fear of traveling or eating out. I am eating healthier now and feel 100% better."

The tabulations of the first 1021 questionnaires showed the diet helped 90.4 percent of those with any of the irritable bowel conditions. This confirmed our belief that diet plays a key role in the cause and treatment of these ailments.

The relationship between irritable bowel symptoms of gas production, chronic or frequent diarrhea, abdominal cramping and rectal irritation to intolerance of certain sugars or wheat gluten is the basis for the colitis diet.

The research diet's development is traced to the author's personal struggles with irritable bowel disease. Like so many, I tried to identify various foods that seemed to exacerbate the symptoms. Unlike most others, I had the benefit of training in both medicine and chemistry. In listing the foods that caused symptoms, I was able to find common chemical elements that have been missed in the past. By identifying these common chemical entities in offending foods, some of the pieces of the puzzle began to fall into place.

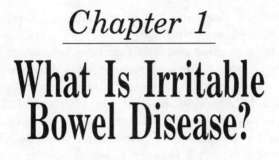

Chapter 1

What Is Irritable Bowel Disease?

Gathering the Clues

Infection has long been suspected as the cause of the irritable bowel diseases (IBD). It has been observed that active inflammatory bowel disease bears many characteristics of infection or parasitic infestation. There is diarrhea; cramping; gas production; malaise; pruritus (rectal itching); mucus, blood and pus in the stool. Extensive efforts have been made to find a bacterial or viral cause for ulcerative colitis, particularly to find some difficult-to-grow, previously unknown exotic microbial agent.

This dilemma was recently expressed by Gary Gitnick, M.D. of the University of California School of Medicine, who wrote in *Drug Therapy*, December 1986:

> Many features of acute Crohn's disease suggest active bacterial infection. These include fever, leukocytosis, abdominal mass, increased erythrocyte sedi-

mentation rate, and increased levels of C-reactive protein and serosomucoids . . . For many years, investigators have presumed that infectious agents, such as bacteria, mycobacteria, or viruses, may play a role in causing or precipitating exacerbations of ulcerative colitis and Crohn's disease. Yet, despite years of study, there is no convincing evidence linking an infectious agent to these diseases. Nonetheless, because of the possible interaction between infectious agents and inflammatory bowel disease (IBD), physicians have used antimicrobial agents empirically in the management of some patients with Crohn's disease or ulcerative colitis.

While they are having their acute attacks, cultures are routinely made on the stools of colitis patients. Invariably, these cultures are reported as showing "no pathogenic organisms." Only the normal bacterial inhabitants of the bowel are seen. One valuable clue to the solution of the problem is that, while ulcerative colitis resembles an infectious disease, no "disease" germs are detectable in the bowel movements of the victims. The idea presented itself that perhaps the "infection" is caused by the bacteria that normally inhabit the bowel, the "normal flora"; that these bacteria could be fermenting undigested sugars that had not been absorbed from the bowel by its owner. Even though affected people fail to digest some sugars, many of the myriads of kinds of bacteria in the colon can. They ferment the sugars, producing chemicals that irritate the bowel and cause inflammation that looks exactly like the infections caused by recognized disease germs!

It is interesting to note that these same normal flora

organisms are responsible for nearly *all* infections of the urinary tract. They are regarded as normal when in the colon, but in the kidneys, they are disease producers! Under some conditions, I reasoned, might they also be disease producers in the colon?

The infection concept is reinforced by the knowledge that attacks of colitis can be prevented or made less severe by taking a poorly absorbed sulfa drug such as Azulfidine. This successful prophylactic measure again suggests that infection is involved in irritable bowel disease—even though no disease germs can be cultured. (In the past, no one had considered that the mischief might be due to the normal, nonpathogenic bacterial inhabitants of the bowel.) Cultures for disease bacteria, immunologic studies and examinations of the stools for parasites, all fail to give any consistent findings to explain these crippling, even fatal, maladies. If the problem is not due to some peculiar infectious agent, perhaps there is an interplay between the normal flora and undigested sugars in the intestinal tract.

Infection must play an important role in irritable bowel disease, but some other factor or factors are involved. Something else must be operating, possibly some toxic element common in many foods (a single food irritant would surely have been discovered long ago). In arriving at the research diet, I reasoned that the cause of irritable bowel disease would most likely be some unsuspected component found in many foods that irritates the bowel.

Dietary Factors

The first clue came from my personal experience. When I was a small lad, my mother gave her children raisins in lieu of candy, rightly believing they were more healthful. After two or three years of scratching the hives between my fingers, I linked the tiny itchy water blisters to eating raisins. Though not fully appreciated at the time, this piece of the puzzle was filed away.

Another important piece of the puzzle came to me some twenty years later, after graduation from medical school. While assisting a surgeon in removing a colon destroyed by ulcerative colitis, the then-intern asked his surgeon mentor what had caused the colitis. The surgeon replied that he did not know, but that he felt orange juice had something to do with it. He explained, "I have had ulcerative colitis patients drink a glass of orange juice while I examine the insides of their colons with a proctoscope and I could see their bowel linings become inflamed right before my eyes." This piece of the puzzle seemed to be lost in the files for several years, but aided in constructing the solution to the mystery.

In adulthood, the progressively annoying symptoms of gas, diarrhea, abdominal cramps and pruritus began plaguing me. I started reading all of the information I could find about irritable bowel diseases. Most authorities had about the same thing to say about it: "We don't know what causes it." Then I began listing the foods that seemed to cause my symptoms. Bananas, oranges and apples were first on the list. Grapes, raisins, watermelon, ice cream and waffle syrup soon followed.

The Known Pieces of the Puzzle

The first step to problem solving is to assemble all of the givens or the known facts about the problem. This entails first reading everything others have observed about it. There are a few well-established pieces of knowledge regarding irritable bowel disease. Literally volumes have been written about the symptoms of ulcerative colitis. These books and articles discuss various manifestations of the malady, complications and suggest nuances of treatment. Often these writers implied that there are different varieties of the disease. A few specialists suspected that these might be variations in the severity and expression of the same ailment.

An excellent article titled: "IBD: Confirming Your Suspicions," by Howard M. Spiro, M.D., professor in the Department of Internal Medicine, Yale University School of Medicine, confirmed my suspicions.

> Specialists argue among themselves whether ulcerative colitis and Crohn's colitis are different disorders. At Yale, we find it impossible to tell them apart by clinical, radiologic, or even pathologic criteria in 25 to 35 percent of patients. (*Diagnosis*, May 1986).

This honesty is most reassuring to the doctors out in the trenches.

Several years ago, colitis investigation started down the right track when it was observed that milk made many ulcerative colitis victims worse. Subsequently, this idea was derailed when it was discovered that the offending element in milk was lactose, the sugar in milk. There followed much interest in lactose intolerance. This intolerance was found to be very widespread, particularly in the non-white races. Among Orientals, Blacks and Native Americans, lactose intolerance occurs in from 50 to 75 percent of the adults!

Many Caucasian adults are also affected. The association of colitis and lactose intolerance was often misinterpreted. Doctors attributed the apparent aggravation of ulcerative colitis by milk to simple lactose intolerance. Because many with ulcerative colitis did not improve when milk was withheld, it was felt that milk intolerance was an ailment distinctly different from ulcerative colitis. Under this concept, those with ulcerative colitis who were lactose intolerant had simply been misdiagnosed. They did not have colitis at all—just lactase deficiency (the enzyme that digests lactose).

This misconception stalled ulcerative colitis research for 30 years. The relationship between lactose intolerance and ulcerative colitis is now scarcely mentioned in medical texts. This clue is "the stone the builders rejected, that has become the chief cornerstone." The failure to convert lactose to glucose in the digestive system is one of the primary causes of the irritable bowel diseases. This observation prompted the author to ask the question: Might not other sugars be similarly involved in irritable bowel disease?

Putting The Puzzle Together

I wondered, what could milk, bananas, orange juice and raisins possibly have in common? Prior to the discovery of lactose intolerance, it was believed that the protein of the milk caused antibody reactions in the bowel wall which were responsible for the irritation. The raisins and oranges probably were not producing antibody reactions as they did not have the large protein content milk had. They did not have lactose either, but they reacted in some of the colitis victims in exactly the same way that milk did. The orange juice, bananas and raisins did have one major component in common. All were very rich in fructose, the natural sugar of sweet fruits. Honey is nearly pure fructose.

These clues prompted the author to try a diet restricting both of these sugars on a group of irritable bowel patients in the Jefferson Memorial Hospital in Alexandria, Virginia. In this group of 32 patients, all responded dramatically. Fructose intolerance had been the missing piece of the puzzle. Who would have suspected something as wholesome as orange juice or apples could be causing bowels to bleed and ulcerate?

Fructose and lactose cause problems when they are not digested and absorbed. They then pass into the lower digestive tract where the normal bacterial residents of the bowel ferment them, making large volumes of gas, alcohol, lactic and acetic acids. These compounds are highly irritating to the intestine and cause inflammation of the bowel. The irritable bowel diseases do relate to infection—because non-pathogenic bacteria ferment the unabsorbed sugars in the digestive tract.

Clues From Kentucky

In 1984, a distraught young mother called *The Saturday Evening Post* for help. Her small son had chronic bloody diarrhea. It was worse whenever he had cake or ice cream. No one had been able to advise her as to what might be bothering him. "He has bloody diarrhea nearly all of the time," she said. Could I possibly help her?

This sounded like ulcerative colitis to me. I suggested the lactose-free, fructose-free diet that had been so successful in the Alexandria experience. A month later she reported that amazing improvement had taken place, but now she had found a new offending agent. Whenever her son brushed his teeth, he would get diarrhea and his bowels would bleed. When questioned about what kind of toothpaste the youngster used, she reported she had tried several of the sugar-free brands believing this would be best for him in light of his intolerance to lactose and fructose. I pointed out to her that all of these preparations are sweetened with sorbitol, a nonabsorbed sugar. Sorbitol behaves in the bowel in exactly the same way the unabsorbed lactose and fructose do.

More months went by and the mother called to report that the tot was doing well but she had discovered that some processed meat products had caused his symptoms to recur. This time, she fingered the guilty agent. Mannitol, yet another indigestible sugar, was causing colitis in her child. At last report, the little boy is free of all symptoms. He is growing and healthy in every way. He still has to carefully limit his ice cream, candy,

DR. GIBBONS'S ULCERATIVE COLITIS/ IRRITABLE BOWEL DIET

The goal of this diet is to sharply limit the amount of the poorly assimilated sugars that may ferment in the bowel and cause gas, diarrhea and irritation. These sugars are: fructose, lactose, mannitol and sorbitol.

FOODS TO BE AVOIDED

Lactose–(the natural sugar in milk) containing foods: Milk, chocolate milk, ice cream, and whey. (Butter and cheese are permitted, as the lactose has been removed in their production. Cottage cheese and yogurt are permitted, as most of the lactose has been removed from them by the fermentation involved in their production.)

FRUCTOSE-CONTAINING FOODS:

Orange juice and any sweet fruits: oranges, apples, pears, grapes, bananas, pineapple, melons, etc.; honey; waffle syrup made with corn sweetener; corn sweetener (in soda pop, pastry, candy, cereals, coffee creamers, salad dressing, sweet pickles ice cream, ham, etc.) READ THE LABELS ON ALL FOODS!

SORBITOL AND MANNITOL CONTAINING FOODS:

Sugarless chewing gum, sugarless candy (diabetic candy), toothpaste, and breath mints. Processed meats may contain sorbitol.

OTHER FOODS TO BE AVOIDED:

Wheat bran, beans, sweet corn, chocolate, chili powder, pepper, and other hot spices.

FOODS PERMITTED

All cereals (rice and corn preferred), breads (white preferred), cheese, butter, meat, fish and poultry. All vegetables with the exception of sweet corn and dried beans. Tomatoes and avocados are recommended. *Small* amounts of cane sugar are permitted.

soda pop and milk, and he scrupulously avoids sorbitol and mannitol.

The colitis research diet restricts lactose, fructose, sorbitol and mannitol. This diet appears to give relief to the majority of those suffering from the irritable bowel diseases, including ulcerative colitis.

My recommendations for the use of the diet: those with active symptoms should avoid the foods that contain any of these sugars. As our studies have shown, a bowel irritated by intolerance of any of these sugars often has impaired ability to handle the others. Those with active fructose intolerance will probably be intolerant of lactose also. Lactose-intolerant individuals with badly irritated colons are likely to be made worse by fructose and they may become intolerant to the gluten in wheat. Many who suffer from celiac disease (intolerance to wheat gluten) will be made worse when they eat lactose or fructose!

As the bowel lining heals, most can again tolerate small amounts of these sugars. They may be able to handle an orange or a banana a day with no symptoms. Foods with high amounts of these sugars, such as ice cream, can start the inflammation of the bowel all over again.

Associated Conditions

"Fat, fair, forty, female" were the "Four Fs" medical students were once taught. These were the findings usually associated with gallstone disease. Soon another F was added for flatulence, which is also associated, and fecund, or fertile (perhaps because it begins with F) was added to the list. The implication was that somehow this constellation of "F" symptoms caused gallstones to form.

It now appears that irritable bowel disease is most often responsible for gallstones and flatulence in fair, fat, fortyish females. The IBD may be due to fructose intolerance, lactose intolerance, gluten intolerance, or combinations of these. Gallstone formation is often a consequence of the irritable bowel disease rather than the cause. To the list I would propose adding other maladies often arising from irritable bowel disease. (Now if someone could only find ways to spell kidney stones, pruritus, arthritis, hemorrhoids and diverticulitis with Fs!)

While giving medical care to military dependents and retirees at Fort Benjamin Harrison in Indianapolis, I have been amazed at how frequently these symptoms are found together in the same patients. Most of the Fort Harrison patients fall into the middle-age group and have a wide variety of ailments, but approximately one out of every 20 patients complains of bloating, chronic diarrhea, flatulence and abdominal cramping pains. A high percentage of these patients have had their gall bladders removed; many have had kidney stones, appendectomies and hemorrhoids (which are almost universal in IBD sufferers)—the whole gamut of intestinal complaints clustering in the same individuals.

In the past, doctors have often looked at each of these conditions as independent problems occurring alone or only coincidentally with the others. In this book, I will attempt to show how many of these conditions interrelate and are traced to faulty digestion of

Anatomy of the Bowel

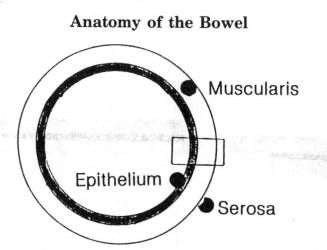

BOWEL CROSS SECTION The bowel is a long tube covered on the outside by a thin membrane called the *serosa*. This layer resembles plastic wrap.

Beneath the serosa is a double layer of muscle. One layer encircles the intestine, the other runs longitudinally. Food is moved along the tube by rhythmic contractions and relaxation of these muscles.

Inside the muscular layer is the *epithelium*. This is a very complex layer. It has the dual role of producing digestive enzymes and absorbing food substances. This lining layer also acts as a protective barrier against unwanted chemicals and microorganisms. The damage to the epithelium by irritable bowel disease may be the reason for the increased susceptibility to cancer of the intestine. This layer is devoid of nerves and severe damage often goes unnoticed.

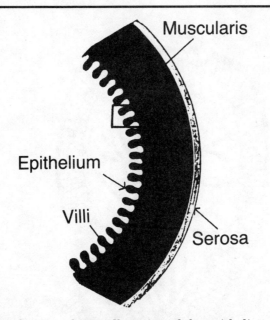

Magnification of a small section of the epithelium of the small bowel reveals myriads of tiny finger-like projections called *villi*. These tiny structures greatly increase the reactive surface area of the intestine. They line only the small bowel and are the working units of the digestive "machinery." In Crohn's disease and celiac sprue, there is extensive damage to the villi that may progress to complete destruction.

sugars and/or wheat gluten. It is an attempt at unification, if you will.

When fructose, lactose or wheat gluten fail to be digested and absorbed, they are fermented by the bacteria in the bowel. This results in a whole chain of chemical events, some with damaging consequences. When exam-

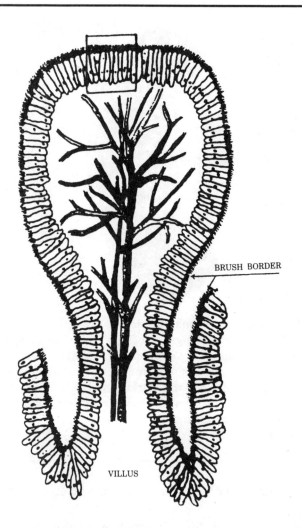

Magnification of a villus reveals a network of blood vessels in its interior and a covering of tall columnar cells.

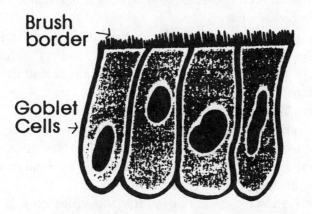

Brush border

Goblet Cells →

A closer look at the columnar cells reveals the "brush border" of these cells covering the surface exposed to the food stream inside the intestine. The brush border is important because many of the digestive enzymes reside on the "bristles" of the "brush."

The brush border is quite fragile. It is easily damaged by infection or chemical insult, and may be suddenly sloughed out. Diarrhea is usually associated with damage to the brush border. Its regrowth depends on the extent of the damage. Mild damage may be repaired in only a few days. Extensive injury may take months to restore. With the loss of the brush border, digestion is impaired. This results in malabsorption. If the irritative process persists, malnutrition will follow.

ining a few of these chemical reactions from a chemist's point of view, the most striking result is the production of large volumes of gas. The fermentation of a quarter pound of one of these sugars produces about 20 quarts of gas (it seems like much more). The gas distends the abdomen and causes the "bloating" and flatulence of irritable bowel disease.

As gases are formed, the carbon dioxide portion is harmlessly absorbed into the blood and is exhaled through the lungs—along with a small amount of hydrogen. The hydrogen and methane produced do not readily dissolve in blood and are passed rectally.

In our modern society, the uninhibited passage of this gas publicly is taboo and many of us go about bloated and suffering from overdistended colons due to large volumes of this retained gas.

This gaseous distention of the intestines crowds the limited space of the abdominal cavity and forces the stomachs of some victims to herniate through the esophageal passage into the chest, which results in a hiatal hernia.

Alcohol, lactic acid, and other chemical byproducts of fermentation irritate the bowel and cause forceful cramping pains. These powerful contractions put the gas trapped in the colon under great pressure. This causes "blow outs" in the thin, weak-walled portions of the' colon, and diverticulosis develops.

Where do I think these new discoveries will lead? First I believe that colectomies will become rare operations. This new knowledge will give new insights into the *prevention and treatment* of several conditions which in the past have been poorly understood. In addition to the irritable bowel diseases, some cases of arthritis will respond to the diet; gallstones and kidney stones may be prevented, as may hemorrhoids, diverticulosis, psoriasis, eczema and perhaps other yet to be discovered medical conditions.

Chapter 2

The Culprits Behind IBS

To understand IBD and IBS a little better, a brief lesson in anatomy is in order.

"Intestinal Diabetes"

Flooding the lower intestinal tract with fructose, lactose, sorbitol, mannitol and wheat bran is in some ways analogous to diabetes. Instead of excessive glucose accumulating in the blood, excessive amounts of these sugars pool in the bowel. With this accumulation, bacterial fermentation occurs. (Even though the individual may lack the enzymes necessary to digest these sugars, some of the myriads of bacterial inhabitants of the bowel are able to metabolize them into gas, alcohol and lactic acid.) The concept of "diabetes of the bowel" is helpful in dietary planning to prevent indigestible sugar overload.

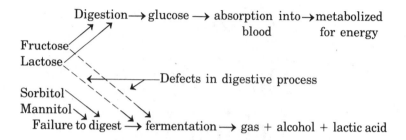

The lactic acid and alcohol produced by the fermentation harshly irritate the bowel resulting in diarrhea, mucus production, bleeding and sloughing of the lining. In irritable bowel diseases, a vicious cycle develops. Lactic acid burns the bowel, causing the enzyme–producing lining to be sloughed out. This further impairs lactose and fructose digestion which, in turn, allows more fermentation to make more lactic acid.

Many individuals who have been diagnosed as having milk allergy or orange juice allergy in the past, should more properly be diagnosed as being lactose or fructose intolerant, rather than allergic. It has long been observed that many adults do not tolerate lactose well, particularly non-Caucasians. Fructose intolerance has not been appreciated as a cause of serious health problems until now. It appears to be the sleeper that has been missed as a causative factor in irritable bowel disease. In this study, it was found to be the most important factor causing bowel irritation.

Ulcerative Colitis

The irritable bowel diseases affect an estimated 2 million Americans (10 percent of whom are children). Estimates vary, but between 10 and 20 percent of the adult population is affected by irritable bowel disease to some degree.

According to the text books, there are several fairly distinct forms of irritable bowel disease. In actuality, the varieties are more alike than they are different. There is considerable debate and confusion as to whether or not ulcerative colitis and Crohn's disease, the major forms of irritable bowel disease, are really different diseases, or if they might not be different expressions of the same pathological process at play in different parts of the intestine.

Ulcerative colitis is the term applied to inflammatory disease of the colon; it is typically characterized by bloody diarrhea. Crohn's disease is defined as a chronic inflammation of the small bowel, characterized by cramping abdominal pains, diarrhea and bowel obstruction. In the author's experience, both respond to a diet devoid of lactose, fructose, mannitol and sorbitol. (Fructose/lactose/sorbitol/mannitol avoidance is helpful for diarrheas from any cause.) This suggests that the conditions are closely related and that the same metabolic flaw is likely to be responsible for both. The respondents to our survey supported this concept as the victims of both diseases reported improvement with the colitis diet.

Ulcerative colitis is the end stage of irritable bowel disease manifested by chronic diarrhea (often bloody), large amounts of mucus in the stool, malnutrition with weight loss, anemia, hair loss, kidney stones, abdominal pain and, commonly, arthritis. In severe attacks of the illness, the victim may have 10 to 20 loose stools per day. These are accompanied by severe cramping pains that produce violent diarrhea with profuse gas production. The urge to defecate is immediate. High fever with severe episodes is not uncommon. When pain is noted, the ulcerative process has eroded the epithelial lining layer and is attacking the deeper muscular layers of the intestinal wall. (The epithelium or mucous membrane lining the hollow of the intestine is largely devoid of sensory nerves, and irritation is not likely to be painful. This is unfortunate because significant damage to the lining may be occurring without the patient being aware of the seriousness of the process.) Pain is an important warning that dangerous bowel disease is present. Mild ulcerative colitis is often diagnosed as irritable bowel syndrome, spastic colitis, mucous colitis or simply as colitis.

Severe ulcerative colitis is fraught with complications in addition to those mentioned above. The ulcers may perforate the colon and spill stool into the abdominal cavity, causing peritonitis. Perforations may also take the form of fistulas, or open passages, tunneling into the vagina or urinary bladder. Other complications include severe liver damage of several kinds: cirrhosis, fatty degeneration and sclerosing angiitis. All are potentially fatal. The inflammatory process may paralyze the colon, causing life-threatening toxic megacolon. Here the loss of the muscular action in the bowel wall results in a ballooning of the colon. The wall becomes dangerously thinned so rupture is possible with subsequent peritonitis and frequently death. Sudden, massive hemorrhage from the bowel may occur with grave consequences. Inflammation of the inner parts of the eyes has been associated with ulcerative colitis, specifically posterior uveitis. Children with significant ulcerative colitis suffer retardation of growth.

Ulcerative colitis greatly predisposes one to cancer of the colon. By the fourth decade with the disease, 70 percent of the patients will have developed cancer of the bowel.

Because of the seriousness of this problem, a colostomy or ileostomy (bringing the small bowel out to an opening in the abdominal wall), is the fate of more than 20,000 Americans annually.

The diagnosis of ulcerative colitis is made by noting a typical pattern on a barium enema x-ray, or by direct visual inspection of the bowel lining by proctoscopic or colonoscopic examination. Open ulcers on the lining are noted with tags, mucous lakes, detached folds (called pseudo-polyps), and passages tunneled beneath the lining. Confirmation of these observations are made by taking biopsy specimens of the involved bowel.

The conventional treatment of ulcerative colitis has consisted of a lactose-free diet, one of the cortisone family of drugs for acute or severe disease, and sulfasalazine, a poorly–absorbed sulfa. The cortisone reduces the inflammatory reaction in the bowel lining. The sulfa inhibits bacterial growth and reduces the alcohol and lactic acid production. For mild disease, Lomotil is helpful in reducing the frequency of stools and pain. (This drug belongs to the narcotic family of pain relievers.)

ULCERATIVE COLITIS The molting or lacy appearance of the inside of this colon is due to the myriads of small open sores or ulcers. This bowel is very painful. The liquid stools are mostly blood and pus.

Care is exercised to avoid drugs such as this one for severe disease. By relieving pain, you may mask dangerous problems. There is suspicion that they may contribute to the development of toxic megacolon. Azothioprine, one of the drugs used for cancer chemotherapy, is also effective in treating some cases of ulcerative colitis.

In our initial survey, 25 of 39 respondents with ulcerative colitis reported excellent results with the lactose/fructose/sorbitol/mannitol-restricted diet. Perhaps avoidance of these sugars may not result in a cure, but any significant means of lessening the destructiveness of this disease is to be regarded as a great advance.

Case Report

A 20-year-old, white, male student presented because of rapid loss of hair. He complained not only of the falling hair, but also of arrested growth of his hair and fingernails for approximately six months. He reported passage of large volumes of gas and four to six liquid stools per day. He had also noted impotence.

Past history: This 193-pound, six-foot-seven-inch man had enjoyed excellent health until six months previously when he began taking erythromycin and tetracycline for acne. It was at this time he began having diarrhea. After stopping the antibiotics, the diarrhea persisted. He began taking a multiple vitamin tablet daily with no improvement. He reported doing his own cooking and listed his diet as cold cereal with milk and sugar plus orange juice for breakfast most mornings.

For lunch, he often had a candy bar or ice cream cone. Dinner consisted of a warmed burrito or TV dinner and a glass of milk. (This had also been his diet prior to the onset of his illness.)

The laboratory findings showed that his hematocrit was 39, hemoglobin 12.4, WBC 10,300, sedimentation rate 18; stool negative for parasites and ova; stool culture: normal flora; stool occult blood: trace; chest x-ray and EKG were normal. Biopsy of the bowel mucosa was reported consistent with ulcerative colitis.

The patient was given 15 mg of prednisone daily for two days. He was started on a lactose/fructose/sorbitol/mannitol–restricted diet. His diarrhea ceased on the fourth day of treatment. Over the ensuing month, his stools decreased to two a day and were formed. He gained eight pounds and his nails grew 4mm while his longest scalp hair grew 12mm. He remains well and active. He continues to avoid these sugars and has a return of his symptoms only when he goes off the diet.

Crohn's Disease

(Granulomatous ileitis, ileocolitis, regional enteritis)

Crohn's disease is an inflammation of the bowel that, by definition, attacks primarily the small bowel. Ulcerative colitis, again by definition, mainly involves the colon or large bowel. Some authorities believe Crohn's and ulcerative colitis to be two distinct conditions; others feel they are different expressions of the same disease process. The symptoms of the two conditions are identical; even the microscopic findings are often confusing.

In some instances, Crohn's disease may involve not only the small bowel, but also the colon and sometimes the stomach and duodenum as well. The inflammatory process may be intense, causing thickening of all layers of the intestinal wall. This may be so severe as to cause the lumen or opening through the intestine to become blocked off. Characteristically, this inflammation hits some areas of the bowel, and skips others. As in ulcerative colitis, because the small bowel lining is rather devoid of nerve cells, severe inflammation may be occurring without the individual being particularly aware of its serious nature. As the lining is eroded, involvement of the deeper layers of the intestine is signaled by pain.

The symptoms of Crohn's disease are indistinguishable from the signs of the other irritable bowel maladies: chronic diarrhea, pain, weight loss, fever, anorexia, etc. The condition may also appear suddenly presenting with an illness that can only be distinguished from appendicitis at surgery. More often, it presents as a chronic problem which comes and goes with severe colic, abdominal distention, constipation and vomiting resulting from partial obstruction of the intestine. Persistence of these problems coupled with malabsorption of food (due to bowel inflammation, loss of digestive enzymes, and the loss of villi and bowel surface area) leads to weight loss and malnutrition.

Many mild forms of this disease go unrecognized and only those with severe cases come to medical attention. The more severe expressions of the disease are devasta-

ting. The erosive processes of the disease will occasionally perforate the bowel wall and form passages or
"sinuses" into other parts of the intestine, the bladder,
vagina, or even through the body wall out onto the skin!
This same erosive process may perforate the intestine
and form abscesses within the abdominal cavity, e.g., in
the pelvis, or under the liver. It may also cause abscesses to form behind the peritoneum, the velamentous
sac lining the abdominal cavity. Obstruction, fistuliza-
tion and abscess formation are common complications of
Crohn's. Less common are intestinal bleeding, perfora-
tion and small bowel cancer. Anal fistulas (tunnels between the colon and the skin separate from the anal
opening), and anal fissures (ulcerated cracks), are noted
in about one-third of the cases. The finding of an anal
fistula is considered presumptive evidence of Crohn's disease. In many, the rectal pathology may be evident years
before the bowel and systemic maladies become apparent.

Crohn's disease has many manifestations that are
not expressed in the gastrointestinal system. Many of
these wax and wane with the severity of the inflammatory processes occurring in the bowel. Commonly accom-
panying Crohn's are arthritis, aphthous stomatitis
(canker sores of the mouth), erythema nodosum (painful
reddened swellings scattered over the body), episcleritis
(eye inflammation), pyoderma gangrenosum (infection
and death of regions of skin) and the recently noted
psoriasis. These complications are twice as likely to
occur if the colon is involved in addition to the small
bowel.

Some extra-intestinal problems that have been found
to accompany Crohn's disease that do not remit and ex-

acerbate in concert with Crohn's activity are *ankylosing spondylitis* (a severe arthritis of the lower spine), and *uveitis* (inflammation of the iris). In children, Crohn's causes growth retardation, abdominal distention, anemia, chronic diarrhea, foul stools, poor resistance to disease, abdominal pain, arthritis and easily broken bones.

Crohn's and other irritable bowel diseases cause excessive absorption of calcium, oxalate, urate, and bile acids. The first three contribute to kidney stone production, the latter to the formation of gall stones. Dr. Howard Spiro, professor of Internal Medicine at Yale University School of Medicine, suggests that the incidence of bowel cancer is increased in persons with Crohn's disease.

The diagnosis is usually established by upper GI and small bowel series x-rays. Frequently, surgery is necessary to relieve bowel obstructions or to drain abscesses that form as a result of Crohn's disease. Often, diseased segments of bowel must be surgically removed or bypassed. Recurrence of the disease occurs in about 95 percent of the cases after surgery. Antibiotics and cortisone are helpful in the acute stages of the disease.

At this time, it is unclear whether failure to digest the sugars of the colitis diet is the cause or the result of Crohn's disease. From our research survey, we had only eight individuals reporting having been diagnosed as having Crohn's disease. Of these, four reported significant benefit from observing the dietary restrictions. This represents 50 percent of Crohn's victims reporting significant improvement by avoiding these sugars.

The majority of the participants in the survey had not been diagnosed as to which type of irritable bowel disease they had. Undoubtedly this group included many with undiagnosed Crohn's. Eighty-five percent of the undiagnosed group reported improvement in their irritable bowel symptoms after trying the diet. All of the author's patients with Crohn's have had excellent responses to the colitis diet.

Celiac Sprue

When the avoidance of lactose, fructose, mannitol and sorbitol fails to stop one's irritable bowel symptoms, one should suspect the symptoms may be due to wheat intolerance, known as celiac sprue. Other causes for failure may be infection, circulatory problems, diabetes, or possibly a tumor.

Celiac disease is one of the less common of the irritable bowel diseases. Its cause is an intolerance to gluten, the protein common to wheat, barley, oats and rye. During World War II, food shortages in Europe afforded clues leading to the discovery of the cause of this condition. It was noticed that a vegetable (mainly potato) diet brought relief to many of those who suffered chronic diarrhea at times when wheat and rye for bread became scarce. Dutch doctors later found that eliminating wheat from the diet caused a marked improvement in many of these individuals.

The definitive test for diagnosing celiac sprue disease is a biopsy of the lining of the small bowel. To do this, a long tube with a capsule-like tip is swallowed. The capsule has a tiny open window and a spring loaded "window sill" knife. When x-rays show the capsule to be in the small bowel, suction is applied to the external end of the tube, pulling a small piece of bowel lining in through the window of the capsule. At the same time, it releases the spring on the miniature knife. As the knife closes the window, it cuts off a small sample of tissue that had been drawn in through the opening. The capsule is then retrieved and the tissue sample removed for study.

Normally, this lining resembles the pile of a carpet with myriads of tiny finger-like projections called villi. In celiac disease, the villi are lost or become short stumps, thereby greatly decreasing the absorptive surface area of the bowel. Also lost are the ends of the cells covering the villi. These cells normally support numerous hair-like projections called the brush border. The brush border is important because many of the digestive enzymes reside on the bristles of the brush. When these are lost, many food substances fail to be digested. Undigested foodstuffs are fermented to produce lactic acid, alcohol and other irritating chemicals that cause diarrhea. The failure to digest food coupled with the rapid transit time of diarrhea, causes the victim to become malnourished. This malabsorption of nutrients in celiac disease closely resembles starvation and the malabsorption seen in ulcerative colitis, Crohn's disease, infections of the bowel and the other irritable bowel syndromes.

Celiac disease is thus related to the other irritable bowel diseases. Celiac victims share many of the problems of these other conditions. When the participants of a celiac–sprue convention were surveyed, one third responded that they were aware that they were lactose intolerant as well as wheat intolerant. A third of those

surveyed had individually discovered that they were
also intolerant of foods containing fructose!

Other surprising findings were the association of arthritis (50 percent), gallstones (50 percent), kidney
stones (20 percent), appendicitis (50 percent) and psoriasis. The occurrence rates of these associated complications were almost identical with those of the other
irritable bowel diseases: ulcerative colitis, Crohn's, spastic colitis, and irritable bowel syndrome.

Many of the respondents to the colitis survey of *The
Saturday Evening Post* volunteered the observation that
wheat bran aggravated their bowel problems. It appears
that many of those who are lactose and fructose intolerant are also bothered by wheat bran the way celiac patients are bothered by fructose and lactose. These
intolerances tend to interrelate, probably reflecting the
loss of the brush border of the bowel lining. In our Colitis Club survey, only three diagnosed celiac sprue patients responded, but two of the three reported they had
been helped by avoiding fructose and lactose as well as
wheat gluten.

Treatment of celiac disease has been a rigorous
avoidance of gluten–containing foods. Victims are permitted the meat and vegetable foods. As mentioned,
one third of these individuals must also avoid lactose
and fructose. There are several organizations for celiac-sprue patients, which are very helpful. The associations give out vital information on what you can eat
with celiac sprue, and where to buy gluten–free foods.
They also provide gluten–free recipes and conduct
highly informative seminars. The associations are
particularly helpful in giving patient information, as

most doctors are not well informed about this rather rare malady. One celiac sprue organization can be contacted at:

Celiac Sprue Association (CSA)/USA
P.O. Box 31700
Omaha, Nebraska 68131-0700 Phone 402-558-0600

Those with "colitis," Crohn's disease, or any of the irritable bowel diseases should be aware of the possibility of their having gluten intolerance. They should avoid the above mentioned cereals if they prove to be irritating to their digestive systems. Persons with any of the irritable bowel diseases, including celiac sprue, should avoid sorbitol and mannitol.

Fructose Intolerance Among Celiac Sprue Victims

Fructose intolerance has not previously been recognized as being associated with gluten intolerance in celiac sprue victims. A survey questionnaire was circulated among the convention participants of the Midwestern Celiac Sprue Association held October 1984. One third of the participants were aware that they were lactose intolerant as well as gluten intolerant, and had restricted their diets accordingly. A nearly equal number had become aware that they did not tolerate foods high in fructose. Many in the survey were aware of "other food allergies." When questions relating specifically to tolerance of these sugars were presented, nearly one third replied that sweet fruits, candy, ice cream, waffle syrup, and other fructose—rich foods caused exacerbations of their disease. No one had previously suggested that this sugar was the common element in the foods they were "allergic to." Eating them evoked symptoms indistinguishable from those of celiac-sprue. These respondents reported that they had discovered their intolerance to fructose rich foods empirically, and they now carefully avoided them in their diets. They did not know these foods had the sugar fructose in common, or that their symptoms were due to this sugar.

See the following pages for lists of foods known to contain gluten and wheat products. Some modifications will have to be made in the gluten–free diet if one is also intolerant of fructose and/or lactose.

Colitis and the Skin

Several skin problems stem from irritable bowel disease. The most studied and best documented is the disease *dermatitis herpetiformis*, a blistering rash that accompanies celiac sprue. When the sprue convention was surveyed, 32 percent reported some kind of skin problems; a surprising 16 percent reported psoriasis. (Recent reports have also linked psoriasis and Crohn's disease.)

Of the first 1,068 respondents to *The Saturday Evening Post* Colitis Club survey, 169 reported they had skin problems, 81 reported psoriasis. Two-hundred-and-four reported improvement after trying the Colitis Club diet for a month. Of the 500 respondents to the Kidney Stone Formers Club survey, 145 reported skin disease!

GLUTEN-FREE DIET

Types of Foods	*Include*	*Avoid*
SOUPS	Homemade broth and unthickened vegetable soups; cream soups prepared with cream, cornstarch, rice, potato, or soy bean flour.	All canned, frozen, or dry soups containing gluten. Bouillon, noodle soups, all commercial thickened soups. Soups containing wheat, rye, oats, and barley.
MEAT and MEAT SUBSTITUTES 3 or more servings	Fresh meat, poultry, seafood, plain unbreaded frozen meats, fish, poultry; fish canned in oil or brine, Swiss cheese, cheddar cheese, Parmesan cheese, pure peanut butter, plain dried beans or peas, eggs, *cottage cheese, (check for vegetable gums). Fried, boiled, scrambled, or poached eggs. All natural cheeses. Imitation cheeses that do not contain prohibited flours. Cheese food. Velveeta.	Prepared meats which contain wheat, rye, oats, or barley, such as: *sausage, *weiners, *bologna, *luncheon meats, *chili, *meatloaf, *hamburger with cereal filler, *canned meat mixtures such as Spam, *sandwich spreads, stews with noodles or dumplings. *Pasteurized cheese spreads. *Canned baked beans. Souffles or omelettes unless prepared with allowed flours. *Tuna canned in vegetable broth and turkey with hydrolized vegetable protein injected as part of the basting solution.

* Some may be used if checked with manufacturer and found to be gluten free.

Note: Brand names are used for clarification only and do not constitute an endorsement.

Types of Foods	Include	Avoid
POTATO and POTATO SUBSTITUTES 1 or more servings	White potato, sweet potato, yams, rice, hominy. AROTEM pasta. Potato chips. Corn chips.	Creamed or escalloped unless prepared with allowed flours. Macaroni, noodles, spaghetti, lasagna, vermicelli. *Commercial potato salad. *Packaged rice mixes.
VEGETABLES	All plain, fresh, frozen, canned (include a dark green or deep yellow daily for a source of vitamin A).	Breaded, creamed, or escalloped unless prepared with allowed flours. *Commercially prepared vegetables or salads.
BREADS	Breads or muffins made from: rice flour (white or brown), corn flour, starch or meal, tapioca flour, potato flour, soybean flour and/or arrowroot flour. Pure corn meal tortillas, gluten-free bread mix.	All bread and bread products containing wheat, rye, barley, oats, bran, buckwheat, graham, wheat germ, malt, millet, kasha or bulgur. All crackers, Ry-Krisp, rusks, zwieback, pretzels. Bread or cracker crumbs. Wheat starch. Bread stuffing. Commercially prepared mixes. Dumplings.

* Some may be used if checked with manufacturer and found to be gluten free.
Note: Brand names are used for clarification only and do not constitute an endorsement.

Types of Foods	Include	Avoid
CEREALS 1 or more servings	Puffed rice; pure corn meal; rice, hominy, Cream of Rice; Kellogg's Sugar Pops; Post Fruity & Cocoa Pebbles. Gluten-free corn flakes, *Rice Krispies, Corn Pops	Snack cereal foods, bran cereals, Cream of Wheat, farina, Grapenuts, oatmeal, shredded wheat, puffed wheat, Ralston, Wheatena, Pablum, wheat germ, buckwheat, *cornflakes. Cereals with malt added.
FATS as desired	Butter, cream, margarine, vegetable oil, vegetable shortening, animal fat, pure mayonnaise, homemade salad dressings and gravies prepared with allowed ingredients.	*Commercially prepared salad dressings and gravies containing gluten stabilizers or thickened with gluten-containing flours. Nondairy creamers.
FRUITS	Fresh, frozen, canned or dried fruits and fruit juices. (Include 1 serving citrus fruit or juice daily for a source of vitamin C.)	Fruits prepared with wheat, rye, oats, or barley. *Thickened or prepared fruits; some pie fillings.
DESSERTS as desired	Homemade cakes, cookies, pastries, pies, puddings, (cornstarch, rice, tapioca) prepared with allowed ingredients. Gelatin desserts, meringues,	Commercial cakes, cookies, pies, doughnuts, pastries, puddings, pie crust; ice cream cones, prepared mixes containing wheat, rye, oats, or barley.

Types of Foods	*Include*	*Avoid*
DESSERTS *(cont.)*	custard, fruit ices and whips.	Icing mixes. *Ice cream and sherbert containing gluten stabilizers (vegetable gums).
MILK 2 or more cups	Fresh, dry, evaporated, or condensed milk; buttermilk, sweat cream. Cocoa made with milk, *sour cream, yogurt (check labels for gums).	Malted milk, some commercial chocolate drinks. Ovaltine. *Some non-dairy creamers.
BEVERAGES	Carbonated beverages, fruit juices (fresh or frozen), Kool-Aid, frozen lemonade concentrate, lemonade, unfortified wine.	Fruit punch powders, cocoa mixes, ale, beer, gin, whiskey, *Postum, *instant coffee.
MISCEL-LANEOUS as desired	Salt (iodized), sugar, honey, jelly, jam, gelatin, molasses, pure cocoa powder, coconut, olives, pure fruit syrup, herbs, extracts, food coloring, cloves, *ginger, nutmeg, cinnamon, cornstarch, yeast, sodium bicarbonate, cream of tartar,	Chili seasoning mix, gravy extracts, *starch, malt, natural flavoring (may contain malt), *hydrolized vegetable protein, *chewing gum, *catsup, *mustard, *soy sauce, *curry powder, horseradish, *vegetable gum,

* Some may be used if checked with manufacturer and found to be gluten free.

Note: Brand names are used for clarification only and do not constitute an endorsement.

Types of Foods	Include	Avoid
MISCEL- LANEOUS *(cont.)*	nuts, dry mustard, sodium glutamate, garlic, pure chili pepper, cider vinegar, wine vinegar, pop- corn, pure chocolate	*pickles, *chili pow- der. *Emulsifiers and stabilizers de- rived from or con- taining wheat, rye, oats, or barley. *Vinegar, distilled vinegar, malt vinegar.

	A Suggested Dietary Pattern	*A Sample Menu*
BREAKFAST	Fruit juice Cereal Meat or Meat Substitute Bread Fat Milk Beverage (optional)	Orange Juice Cream of Rice Poached Egg Rice Bread Margarine Milk

NOON MEAL	Soup (optional)
	Meat or Meat
	  Substitute
	Bread
	Vegetable
	Fat
	Fruit and/or Dessert
	Milk
	Beverage (Optional)
		Homemade Chicken
		  Rice Soup
		Tuna Fish
		Gluten-free Soy Bread
		Carrot sticks
		Pure Mayonnaise for
		  Tuna Fish
		Apple
		Milk

Types of Foods	Include	Avoid
EVENING MEAL	Meat or Meat Substitute	Roast Beef
		Mashed Potatoes
	Potato or Potato Substitute	Green Beans
		Sliced Tomato
	Vegetable	Rice and Corn Muffin
	Salad	Margarine
	Bread	Homemade Rice
	Fat	Brownies
	Fruit and/or Dessert	Milk
	Beverage	
NIGHT NOURISH-MENT	Beverage	Lemonade
	Bread and/or Fruit	Banana

I have personally treated several individuals who had eczema that resisted all other therapies. I had these patients follow the colitis diet. No other treatment was given. These patients had dramatic relief of their skin problems.

The diet will not help everyone with a skin disorder. It will help a significant number of those with underlying irritable bowel disease, who have not been helped by other forms of treatment.

Lactose

One of the most common causes of irritable bowel disease is lactose intolerance. The milk of all species of mammals contains this sugar. Whether the milk is dried, canned, skimmed (taking away the fat does not remove the sugar), homogenized, vitamin D enriched, etc., it contains lactose. This sugar has a low order of sweetness, and low solubility. (It is the sandy granular substance noted in stale ice cream.) Many people are unable to convert this sugar into glucose, the natural sugar of the blood that the body uses as its principal fuel. Unconverted, it remains in the intestinal tract where its fermentation causes irritation of the lining of the bowels. Bacterial fermentation changes the lactose into carbon dioxide which is absorbed into the blood and escapes the body through the lungs, water that is excreted through the kidneys, hydrogen and methane which are passed as flatus, lactic acid and alcohol which harshly irritate the mucosa of the lower digestive tract.

Lactose is a disaccharide. It is formed by the joining of a molecule of glucose and a molecule of galactose. The conversion of lactose to glucose so it can be accepted into the body's energy reactions depends on two chemical processes. The first is the separation of the glucose and galactose. The second involves the conversion of the galactose into glucose. Failure to complete either one of these chemical reactions may lead to lactose intolerance.

The ability to digest lactose is often lost in middle age. The loss is noted by individuals experiencing the formation of large volumes of intestinal gas which may be accompanied with loose stools, blood in the stool, and abdominal cramping. About 75 percent of the world's adult population do not tolerate lactose well. Orientals, Native Americans, and Blacks tend to have this milk intolerance. Most Caucasians tolerate it in adulthood, but many do not. Many tolerate small amounts, but bloat when larger amounts of milk are taken.

Not infrequently, babies are unable to digest lactose. These infants may have colic, chronic diarrhea, malabsorption, failure to thrive, bronchitis, snuffling or bubbly respirations, abdominal pain, frequent crying, respiratory infections and a mousey body odor. They do well on lactose–free diets such as lactose–free formula or soybean formula. Some do well on milk treated with Lactaid.

Not all products made from milk contain lactose. In the production of many milk products, the lactose is removed. Those who are intolerant of milk need not avoid cheese, butter, or cottage cheese. In the production of butter, the water soluble lactose remains in the buttermilk residue after the butter fat is removed. The lactose remaining in the butter is negligible and those with irritable bowel disease or lactose intolerance have no problems eating butter.

Likewise when rennin is added to milk, casein (protein) curds which are used to make cheese form. As the curds are removed from the milk, the water soluble lactose remains behind in the whey. The curds are then washed with water and more of the lactose is removed. It is true that the small amount remaining can ferment to make lactic acid which is responsible for the taste of "sharp" cheese. But the amount of lactose present is relatively small and unimportant. The liquid whey that is removed from the cheese is largely a solution of lactose and should be avoided by lactose intolerant individuals.

Lactose is removed by fermentation in the production of cottage cheese. The cream or fat is first removed from the milk, as the fat prevents curd formation. Lactobacilli are added to the skim milk and produce lactic acid by fermenting the lactose. This acid causes the milk to curdle. When cottage cheese is made, the curds are washed and unfermented lactose is removed. Salt and a small amount of sour cream are added for flavor to complete the process. In yogurt production, the fermentation process is allowed to go on to convert as much of the lactose as possible to lactic acid. Hence the strong acid flavor of yogurt. Both of these products are usually tolerated by those who are lactose intolerant, even though yogurt contains some lactose.

Vast numbers of lactobacilli are present in both cottage cheese and yogurt. These bacteria produce the enzyme lactase necessary to split and digest lactose. These foods have been found to actually improve lactose tolerance, as the bacterial lactase replaces the lacking enzyme in breaking down lactose that may have been eaten.

For individuals who are intolerant of lactose but are not bothered by fructose, one tablespoon of non-dairy coffee creamer stirred into a glass of water makes a good milk substitute. This works particularly well for use with cereal.

Powdered milk has all of the lactose of whole milk and should be avoided by those who are intolerant of lactose. However, non-dairy creamer contains corn sweetener which will cause bowel irritation in those who are fructose intolerant.

Commercial lactase is now available under the trade names of Lactaid and Lactrase. This may be added to milk to perform the digestive step lactose intolerant individuals are unable to accomplish. It may also be taken in tablet form as milk and lactose rich foods are eaten. The product works well, and those with mild disease may find this to be a good solution to their problem. For those with active ulcerative bowel disease, prudence would call for the avoidance of lactose rather than using the enzyme replacement.

A very similar condition exists where the affected person cannot tolerate the sugar fructose (discussed later). Intolerance to both of these sugars is often present in ulcerative bowel disease. The conditions may exist independently or together. In milder forms of irritable bowel disease, intolerance to one sugar may be relatively more severe. With active disease, it is best to avoid both sugars. Each person must do a little detective work on his own to find out which of the sugars he or she cannot digest. The way to tell if you are milk intolerant is to drink a quart of milk. If it causes you to form large amounts of intestinal gas, you may assume that you are not digesting and assimilating the lactose. If two or three glasses of orange juice cause gas to form, you may assume that you are not digesting fructose. Gas production or loose stools are the simplest clues that you are sugar intolerant.

Tolerance/intolerance for these sugars is genetically determined. In many individuals, lactose intolerance appears soon after birth. It is manifested in colic, fretfulness, diarrhea, gas production, respiratory infections and failure to thrive. This intolerance tends to disappear at about one year of age, become inapparent or partial for many years, only to reappear in adult life. Intolerance to these sugars may be inapparent until the lining of the bowel becomes injured by drugs or infection. Many of the antibiotics injure the bowel mucosa, leaving sugar intolerance in their wake. Likewise, infection by protozoans such as amoebic dysentery organism or giardiasis may render the bowel sugar intolerant.

Galactosemia

Some babies suffer mental retardation when they are able to separate the glucose from the galactose in milk sugar, but fail to convert the galactose into glucose. Galactosemia results when the galactose accumulates throughout their bodies. In most hospitals, newborn babies are routinely tested for this defect. Galactosemia is characterized by elevated blood galactose, coma, cataracts, seizures, hepatosplenomegaly, jaundice and failure to thrive.

Undiagnosed, many affected babies die in the first few months of life as a result of septicemia (bacterial infection in the blood). Others die between two and three years of age as a result of cirrhosis of the liver. Survivors are usually mentally retarded. The treatment for this malady is to raise the affected children on milk substitutes, avoiding all lactose in their diets.

For the lactose restricted diet see page 9.

Infant Colic

Incessant or excessive crying by a small baby often indicates lactose intolerance. If one carefully observes the child, one will note that he or she cries from abdominal pain. The small one may be actually suffering from irritable bowel syndrome! Babies cry almost continually until they are placed on a soybean or other formula that does not contain lactose. As long as their digestive systems are being flooded with indigestible sugar, they will continue to cry. During their first few weeks, babies are fed only milk, and lactose intolerance is the most common cause of colic. (There is lactose in breast as well as in cows' milk, and the insistence on breastfeeding a baby that is having diarrhea may be injurious to the child.) Allergy to milk is usually not allergy at all, but a failure to convert the lactose in the milk to glucose. As the infant begins to have intestinal fermentation, he or she gets cramping pains from the lactic acid irritating the bowels.

Later when orange juice and other fruit juices are given, or when the baby is fed foods sweetened with corn sweetener (including some soy formulas), the infant may develop colic from fructose intolerance. Do not disregard colic as insignificant; the baby is having pains most likely from the failure to digest one or more of the sugars. With the resulting bowel irritation, there is malabsorption, and the child may show retardation of physical and mental growth. Some babies go on to develop the full blown expression of ulcerative colitis, if not checked. Infants should be watched for intolerance to fructose as well as lactose. Allergy to orange juice or apricots may produce colic symptoms just as lactose does. (Babies and small children should never be given fructose in the form of honey. Honey often contains a botulism-like toxin which has been responsible for infant deaths.)

Babies who cry excessively, and those who have tense abdomens or who fail to thrive must have prompt medical attention. Do not attempt to play doctor because you have read some books.

Sucrose

Cane and beet sugars are sucrose. This is a natural sugar that has been separated from pulps of the respective plants. It is refined only in the sense that impurities have been removed. It is, nonetheless, a natural sugar. (The only difference between beet and cane sugars is the trace impurities in each.) Generally, sucrose is tolerated better than lactose or fructose by irritable bowel victims although it is troublesome for those who are fructose intolerant.

Like lactose, sucrose is a disaccharide. This means its molecule is formed by the joining together of the molecules of two simple sugars. One molecule is glucose; the other is fructose. Like lactose, it requires two steps in its digestion. First, the separation of the glucose and fructose. Second, the conversion of the fructose to glucose. (Fructose, lactose, sucrose and starch are all converted to glucose before the body absorbs and uses them for fuel.) Virtually all people have the enzymes necessary to separate sucrose into its simple sugars. Because of its fructose constituent, sucrose troubles many with IBD, but usually to a lesser degree than other fructose sources. One would anticipate irritable bowel problems from sucrose equal to those of fructose because of its fructose component, but sucrose seems to be better tolerated than other sources of fructose. Just why the fructose portion does not cause more bowel irritation is as yet unclear. An educated guess is that as sucrose is hydrolyzed (the process of separating the glucose and fructose), the conversion of the fructose into glucose is facilitated.

According to the Food and Drug Administration, the word sugar is supposed to indicate sucrose when it is used in product ingredient lists. Unfortunately, this is not strictly enforced. Many manufacturers list sugar as an ingredient when they are actually using corn sweetener. Strictly speaking, corn sweetener is sugar, but in view of the discovery that the fructose in corn sweetener often causes irritable bowel syndrome, regulations requiring corn sweetener to be listed as such on labels need to be enforced. The Food and Drug Administration has been informed of this problem. It will take letters from many individuals who have fructose intolerance to spur the administration to take action. The initial correspondence to the Food and Drug Administration informing them of this problem and their reply appear on the following pages.

Common table sugar is sucrose. It is used in coffee, home cooking, canning and candy making. Cane sugar is used in making some commercial candies such as Hershey's and Nestle's chocolate bars. Candies imported from Europe are made from beet sugar, rather than the corn sweetener used in American candy. Most irritable bowel patients can tolerate small amounts of sucrose sweets and may better tolerate imported candies.

Indianapolis, Indiana
May 12, 1986

Mr. John M. Taylor, Director
Division of Regulatory Guidance
Bureau of Foods
Food and Drug Administration
PHS, DHHS
Washington, D.C. 20204

Dear Mr. Taylor:

Over the past four years I have been involved in medical research in the field of ulcerative colitis and irritable bowel syndromes. I have personally treated more than 50 individuals with an irritable bowel disease. My studies have demonstrated that fructose, lactose, sorbitol and mannitol intolerance has been a key factor in provoking most irritable bowel diseases. Lactose and sorbitol have been recognized as causes of bowel irritation for some time. It had not been previously recognized that fructose intolerance was a key element in inciting these diseases. By avoiding these sugars, so far, all of my personal patients have enjoyed dramatic relief from their ailments. Sucrose does not seem to bother these individuals.

I am writing to you regarding a problem that many of my colitis victims, who have had success with this diet, complain to me about. Since corn sweetener is used in so many foods, it is very difficult to avoid fructose. By reading the labels on foods, they can eliminate most of it from their diets. There is a serious problem for them when corn sweetener in the food is listed as "sugar" in the table of ingredients. I would like to suggest that corn sweetener be identified as "corn sweetener" and not as "sugar" in the list of ingredients in commercial foods. I realize the labels in question are technically correct—

corn sweetener and fructose are sugar—but eating fructose unawares does create serious health problems for a great many people who have irritable bowel disease.

My position at *The Saturday Evening Post* is Director of Clinical Research. To conduct our irritable bowel disease study, we invited readers suffering from this group of maladies to write for a lactose/fructose/sorbitol/mannitol–free diet and a questionnaire to be filled out after trying and evaluating the diet. So far, 11,000 have responded. The returned questionnaires have indicated that 85 percent of those trying the diet have experienced relief from their irritable bowel disease. I am including typical letters we have received with returned surveys.

For most people, corn sweetener seems to be perfectly acceptable as a food flavoring. It is only the 5 to 10 percent of the population (mostly in the middle and geriatric age groups), who do not tolerate fructose and develop irritable bowel disease from it. This problem is extremely common. I would like to suggest that in the future foods be marked as lactose free or fructose free by some coding similar to that use to indicate kosher. The incidence of the irritable bowel diseases has been rising over the past decade. I expect to show the increasing incidence of irritable bowel disease parallels the increasing consumption of corn sweetener.

Sincerely Yours,

De Lamar Gibbons, M.D.
Director of Clinical Research
The Saturday Evening Post
1100 Waterway Blvd.
Indianapolis, IN 46202

De Lamar Gibbons, M.D.
Director of Clinical Research
The Saturday Evening Post
1100 Waterway Boulevard
Indianapolis, Indiana 46206

Dear Dr. Gibbons:

This is in reply to your letter of May 12, 1986, concerning ingredient labeling of food to clearly indicate the presence of "corn sweetener," sugar, and/or fructose. We also acknowledge receipt of your letter of May 13, 1986 which included letters you have received from people who have tried your "Colitis diet."

Under the food labeling provisions of the Federal Food, Drug, and Cosmetic Act, the label of a food which is fabricated from two or more ingredients must bear a statement of ingredients in terms of specific common or usual name. The word "sugar" in a statement of ingredients refers solely to "sucrose." Foods which contain fructose, mannitol, sorbitol, etc. may not simply declare "sugar," but must declare the specific name of the individual ingredient used in the product.

"Corn sweetener" is the broad collective term used to refer to a large and rather complex group of corn-derived sweeteners, including corn syrup. The food labeling provisions of the law require a declaration of the ingredients by specific name (e.g., "corn syrup") and not a collective name (e.g., "corn sweetener" or "sugar"). There are, however, some exceptions to this general requirement, such as in the case of certain standardized foods, the regulations for which allow use of the term "corn sweetener" for declaration of the presence in the food of a sweetener derived from corn.

Your suggestion that foods be marked as lactose free or fructose free would likely require the issuance of regulations requiring such labeling on foods. A regulation proposed by an interested person should be submitted in the form of a citizen petition as discussed in regulation 21 CFR 10.30 and must contain facts demonstrating reasonable grounds for the proposal and substantially show that the proposal is in the public interest and will promote the objectives of the Federal Food, Drug, and Cosmetic Act and the Food and Drug Administration. The enclosed information sheet describes how to obtain FDA regulations.

We hope this information is helpful to you.

Sincerely yours,

Eugene R. Leger
Assistant to the Director
Division of Regulatory Guidance
Center for Food Safety
and Applied Nutrition

Enclosure:
How to Obtain FDA Regulations

Fructose

Fructose intolerance has been the missing link in the irritable bowel disease puzzle. Its manifestations are nearly identical to those of lactose intolerance. The role of fructose in bowel disease has not been entertained in the past. Who would suspect that anything so wholesome as orange juice might be so devastating to the bowel lining as to destroy it and necessitate removal of the colon and the establishment of an ileostomy opening in the abdomen?

Fructose is the natural sugar in sweet fruits. Honey is a rather pure form of fructose. The sweetness in apples, pears, pineapples, peaches, plums, melons, oranges, grapefruit, etc., is due to the presence of fructose. These are the natural sources of fructose. Man has learned to chemically make this sugar from corn. The corn is treated with enzymes to make synthetic honey called corn sweetener or corn syrup. Sometimes it is listed in food contents as sugar. It is a sugar, but since many people have fructose intolerance, it is hoped that eventually foods made with this product will be so labeled. This is a particularly insidious source of fructose and it is included in thousands of commercially produced foods, such as ice cream, candy, waffle syrup, jams, jellies, glazes on bakery and cereal products, and soda pop!

This sugar is twice as sweet as cane or beet sugar (sucrose), and many times sweeter than lactose. This may be great for those who are weight conscious, as they need consume only half as many calories of this sugar to get the same sweetness as they would get using cane sugar. For most people, fructose is a perfectly safe wholesome food, but it is not good for those with irritable bowel syndrome or ulcerative colitis.

Most people can convert fructose into glucose and burn it for energy. Others are unable to convert it and, as a result, do not absorb it into their blood. The fructose remains in the bowel where bacteria ferment it to produce carbon dioxide, hydrogen and methane gases, water, alcohol and lactic acid. The two latter substances irritate the bowel lining.

Not everyone with irritable bowel disease is intolerant of fructose. There are some who tolerate it well and others who have intolerance only when the bowel is acutely inflamed or irritated (as by lactose, sorbitol, mannitol, drugs or infection.)

Some have a good tolerance for small amounts of it but have serious symptoms after large doses. The irritated bowel then fails to digest other foods, such as lactose or wheat. As these foods fail to be digested and assimilated, they in turn are fermented. Acid, alcohol and gases resulting from this fermentation further irritate the bowel lining and impair digestion.

No product comparable to Lactaid is available for fructose intolerance. There is nothing you can add to your diet that will facilitate the conversion of fructose to glucose.

Honey From the Corn

An important new source of fructose has been quietly introduced into our diets. A process for making fructose from corn (corn sweetener), has revolutionized the sugar industry. It is less expensive to produce than cane sugar and it is twice as sweet. It has been substituted for cane and beet sugars in waffle syrup, ice cream, candy, commercial pastries, cereals, coffee creamers, salad dressings and soda pop. You do not have to drink orange juice to get fructose toxicity. For most people, fructose is a good wholesome food. Most individuals can turn fructose into glucose and burn it for energy with no difficulty. Because it is twice as sweet as cane sugar, only half as much of it is required for the same desired sweetness. Those who are weight conscious need take in only half as many calories in their favorite sweet dishes. The health food industry touts fructose as "nature's energy sugar." This is a meaningless claim. Tests show it to be absorbed far more slowly than other sugars because of the necessity for its conversion to glucose. In those with irritable bowel problems, much of it fails to be converted and passes into the colon where it is available for fermentation. Among those who cannot digest fructose, some suffer serious bodily harm from it.

In the hospital study, it was noted that many have a partial intolerance to fructose and lactose. This suggests a threshold phenomenon. Some tolerate small amounts of them with no apparent ill effects. When larger amounts are ingested, gas, diarrhea, cramping and rectal irritation ensue. No fructose or lactose is to be permitted during active irritable bowel disease. Once the bowel lining has become irritated, even small amounts of these sugars exacerbate the symptoms.

FRUCTOSE-FREE DIET:
FOODS TO AVOID

Foods containing CORN SWEETENERS

MEATS

Bologna
Frankfurters
Pork and Beans
Meat cooked in barbecue
   Sauce

DRINKS

Coca-Cola
7-Up
Dr. Pepper
Pepsi-Cola
Mountain Dew
Orange Crush
Grape Crush
All other *non-diet* soft drinks

MISCELLANEOUS

Ketchup
Kool-Aid (regular)
TQ Thirst Quencher
Fruit juices (except tomato)
Tang
Coffee-Mate
All waffle syrups
Smucker's jams and syrups
Knott's jams and syrups

MISCELLANEOUS

Swiss Miss Hot Cocoa Mix
Pantry Fresh Sour Cream
   Substitute
Betty Crocker Cake Icing
Natural fructose sugar
Fructose
Graham crackers
Most commercial cookies
Raisins
Most commercial candies
Newman's Own Spaghetti
   Sauce
Ragu Chunky Gardenstyle
   Spaghetti Sauce
Ragu Old World Spaghetti
   Sauce
Prego Plus Ground Beef &
   Onion Spaghetti Sauce
Prego Flavored with Meat
   Spaghetti Sauce
Prego Mushroom Spaghetti
   Sauce
Kraft Russian Salad Dressing
Wishbone French Dressing
Wishbone Italian Dressing
Wishbone Russian Dressing
Maple syrup

All cereals containing CORN SWEETENER

Kellogg's OJs
Kellogg's Honeynut
  Cornflakes
Kellogg's Apple Raisin Crisp
Kellogg's Fruitful Bran
Kellogg's Just Right
Kellogg's Bran Flakes
Kellogg's Raisin Bran
Kellogg's Special K
Kellogg's Corn Pops
Kellogg's Honey Smacks
Kellogg's Cornflakes
Kellogg's Cracklin' Oat Bran
Kellogg's Product 19
Kellogg's Raisin Squares
Kellogg's Marshmallow
  Krispies
Kellogg's Fruit N' Fiber
Kellogg's Frosted Krispies
Kellogg's Cocoa Krispies
Kellogg's Rice Krispies
Kellogg's All-Bran
Kellogg's All-Bran Extra
  Fiber
Post Corn Flakes

Post Raisin Bran
Post Bran Buds
Post Super Sugar Crisp
Post Honey Dip
Post Cocoa Pebbles
Frankenberry
Count Chocula
Fiber One
Cinnamon Crisp
Cinnamon Toast Crunch
Golden Grahams
Circus Fun
Rocky Road
Kaboom
PacMan
Smores
Granola Dippers
Granola Cereal
Peanut Butter Whips
Quaker 100% Natural Cereal
Crispy Wheats
Lucky Charms
Raisin Nut Bran
Trix
Boo Berry

Other products containing CORN SWEETENER

Vick's Cough Silencer
Mediquel
Chloraseptic
Pine Brothers Cough Drops
Victor's Cough Drops
Hall's Mentho-lyptus
Tenys Antacid
Baby Ruth Bars

Doublemint Gum
Freedent Gum
Freshenup Gum
Juicy Fruit Gum
Spearmint Gum
Certs
LifeSavers
Bit-O-Honey

Mounds
Rollo Caramels
Snickers
3 Musketeers

Tootsie Roll
Clark
Oh Henry

Virtually all commercial candy except imported candy and Hershey's and Nestle's chocolate.

PERMITTED FOODS

* All starred foods list sugar as an ingredient. According to FDA rules, this should indicate cane or beet sugar. This rule has not been strictly enforced and in many instances, corn sweetener is listed as sugar. Those without stars are made without sugar or corn sweetener.

All Unprocessed Meats, Fish, & Poultry and Oscar Mayer Ham

Permitted Drinks

Sugar-Free Cocoa Mix
Nestle Quik*
Carnation Sugar Free Hot
  Cocoa Mix
Nestle Hot Cocoa Mix*
Crystal Light Drink
Kool-Aid (sugar-free & add
  sugar)
DOQ Artificial Egg Nog

Sugar Free Ovaltine (con-
  tains lactose)
Diet Coke
Diet Pepsi
Diet 7-Up
Diet Slice
Hershey's Chocolate Milk*
Unsweetened Wyler's Punch
Kraft Instant Malted Milk*
V8

Permitted Cereals

Instant Quaker Oatmeal*
Apple Jacks*
Froot Loops*
King Vitamin*
Smurfberry Crunch
Almond Delight
Bran Chex*

Grape-Nuts
Grape-Nuts Flakes*
Post Fortified Oat Flakes*
Cookie Crisp*
GI Joe*
Sun Flakes
Quaker Shredded Wheat

Life*
100% Bran*
Corn Chex*
Muffin Crisp*
Peanut Butter Crunch*
Capt'n Crunch*
Nabisco Shredded Wheat
Nabisco Shredded Wheat 'n
  Bran
Nabisco Shredded Wheat
  Spoon Size

Corn Bran*
Quaker Puffed Rice
Wheaties*
Country Corn Flakes*
Total*
Kix*
Cheerios*
Total Corn Flakes
All Grains

Permitted Miscellaneous

Molasses
Betty Crocker Frosting Mix
Cornmeal
Softasilk Cake Mix
Duncan Hines Cake Mix*
Kraft Thousand Island
  Dressing*
Catalina French Dressing*
Kraft Bacon and Tomato
  Dressing
Kraft Italian*
Kraft French Dressing*
Kraft Thousand Island
  Dressing*
Wishbone Dijon*
Wishbone Blue Cheese*
Jell-O*
Nestle Butter Scotch*
Royal Gelatin Sugar Free
Royal Gelatin Dessert*
Extra (gum)

Pantry Fresh Buttermilk
  Substitute
Campbell's Pork and Beans*
Ragu Home Style Spaghetti
  Sauce
Peanut Butter*
Tomato Juice—Campbell's,
  Stokley's, Libby's
Fiberall
Sugar Free Metamucil
Dynamints*
Nestle Chocolate*
Hershey's Chocolate*
Peak Toothpaste
Pepsodent Toothpaste
Scope Mouthwash
Listermint with Fluoride
  Mouthwash
Cepacol Mouthwash
Chooz Antacid
Tums Antacid
Gaviscon II Antacid

Glucose

Glucose is the most common sugar in nature, but it seldom occurs in simple form. More commonly it occurs in long chains as starch or cellulose. Starch and cellulose are formed by removing water from glucose:

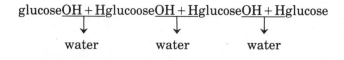

= starch or cellulose, depending on the length of the chains.

Glucose is the gasoline of the human body. The digestive process adds water to starches and reconverts them into glucose. Starch is not absorbed into the blood as such; it must first be changed to glucose. Impaired burning of glucose occurs in diabetes; the sugar then accumulates in the blood and spills into the urine.

Glucose is a particularly attractive fuel. It burns cleanly into carbon dioxide and water. The products of its combustion are harmless to all tissues. There are no waste residues that may accumulate in the body. Brain cells selectively burn only glucose as fuel. This places the cells at risk for deprivation of fuel. Serious injury results when the brain is deprived of this fuel for even a few minutes. These cells benefit from this fuel selectivity, however, as the lack of residue in its combustion allows the cells to function often for more than a hundred years.

Artificial Sweetening Agents

Artificial sweeteners fall into two categories: The non-absorbable sugars, and the synthetic chemical sweeteners. Sorbitol and mannitol are non-absorbable sugars. They are used in diabetic candy, in sugarless chewing gum, toothpaste, antacids, calcium supplements and breath mints. These agents are really sugars, and the label "sugarless" applied to products containing them is technically fraudulent. These sugars are important because they are extremely irritating to the sensitive bowel. There is a dose relationship for these irritants; the larger the dose, the greater the degree of irritation. As with other poorly absorbed sugars, they may be tolerated in small amounts, but should be religiously avoided when the bowel has been irritated. Large amounts of these sugars should be avoided by all. (See page 8 for the account of the child who was so sensitive to minute amounts of these sugars in toothpaste that it caused his bowels to bleed.)

The synthetic chemical sweeteners include cyclamate, saccharin and aspartame. Cyclamate has been removed from the market. (Probably wrongfully, in my opinion. Tests on rodents involved monumental doses. Rodents eventually develop cancer without artificial agents, hence such tests are generally invalid.) Saccharin and aspartame are tolerated well by most irritable bowel victims. The amounts of these substances used is very small because they are so potent at imparting the sweet taste. The use of artificial sweeteners is recommended particularly in soda pop and foods that would normally be sweetened with corn sweetener. The long-term effects of these agents are unknown.

SORBITOL AND MANNITOL-FREE DIETS

MISCELLANEOUS PRODUCTS TO AVOID

Sorbitol-Containing Products

Aim Toothpaste
Osco Gel Toothpaste
Gleem Toothpaste
Topol Toothpaste
Fact Toothpaste
Aquafresh Toothpaste
Checkup Toothpaste

Shane Toothpaste
Pepsodent Toothpaste
Colgate Toothpaste
Close-Up Toothpaste
Crest Gel Toothpaste
Crest Pump Toothpaste
Pearl Drops Toothpaste

Cough Drops

Nice Coughdrops
Cepastat Coughdrops

Antacids

Tempo Antacid
Maalox Plus Antacid
Alka-Mints Antacid

Chewing Gums & Mints

Trident Chewing Gum
Care Free
Velamints

Foods

Frosted Mini-Wheats
Weight Watcher's Salad Dressing
Cory's Low Calorie Syrup

MANNITOL-CONTAINING PRODUCTS

Pepto-Bismol
Mylicon 80
Mylanta II
Theracal

Trident Chewing Gum
Chewels
Care Free Gum

Chapter 3

The Manifestations of Irritable Bowel Syndrome

Irritable Bowel Disease, Spastic Colitis, Mucous Colitis

These terms are generally used interchangeably. They are descriptive terms for the symptom complex of a tendency to diarrhea, abdominal pains, and excessive gas production. No tests definitively establish a diagnosis of one as opposed to any of the others. There are no microscopic findings characteristic of any one of them. In all likelihood, the symptom complex is due to mild expressions of ulcerative colitis, Crohn's disease or celiac sprue.

Individuals with the irritable bowel syndromes respond well to the Colitis Club Diet. Our canvass of individuals trying the diet showed that in most instances, intolerance to one or more of these sugars was the pro-

voking factor for their irritable bowel disease. Individuals with any of the irritable bowel conditions should
avoid sorbitol and mannitol and, when their disease is
acutely active, they should avoid lactose and fructose as
well.

The Reaction Delay Factor

The identification of foods that cause irritable bowel disease is made difficult by the time lapse between eating
a food, and the appearance of symptoms. The delay may
range from 10 to 24 hours. It is hard to relate the milk
or ice cream eaten yesterday with the gas and diarrhea
experienced today, but this is the usual picture. It takes
the unabsorbed sugars several hours to reach the lower
digestive tract where the fermentation occurs.

Pruritus Ani (rectal itching)

Pruritus ani belongs to the irritable bowel family of disorders. It may be the sole expression of digestive failure
or, more often, it is a symptom of more serious internal
disease. When regarded as an independent entity, it is
most often misdiagnosed as hemorrhoids, and is treated
with medications intended for that condition. When recognized as a symptom, it is a common element of any
of the irritable bowel syndromes.

Pruritus ani is most commonly due to lactic acid
leaking from the colon onto the skin surrounding the
anus. This produces intense itching and often pain and

bleeding. Temporary relief follows showering when the leaked material from the bowel is washed away. The cause of the lactic acid production is usually the failure to digest fructose, lactose, sorbitol or mannitol. Fructose has been the most common offender seen in the author's practice. Most often, pruritus follows the eating of bananas, apples, oranges or orange juice, or ice cream. It is important to point out that the intense irritation experienced by this small area of skin suggests that even more severe irritation is occurring internally in the tissues lining the bowel. (As previously mentioned, the bowel lining is nearly devoid of pain nerve endings, so the true extent of the damage occurring in the intestinal wall is not noticed by the victim.)

Pruritus is not an insignificant annoyance to be ignored. It is often the only warning of a more serious internal disease such as Crohn's disease or ulcerative colitis. In a recent report from Russia, one investigator found the occurrence of pruritus among victims of colon cancer to be near 100 percent. This does not say that pruritus causes bowel cancer, but that both share some common inciting factor or factors, and that pruritus may not safely be disregarded. Pruritus suggests that one is at risk for bowel cancer.

The immediate short–term treatment of pruritus is aimed at stopping the itching. Gentle washing of the anal area with soap and water gives immediate relief from pruritus. (Note that washing does not relieve thrombosed hemorrhoids.) Analgesic medications designed to treat hemorrhoids are to be avoided as they themselves are often irritating.

Topical corticosteroids relieve itching for a short

while. These include: Vioform-HC, Mycolog, Vytone, Hytone, Kenalog, Cordran and the over–the–counter preparations such as Cortaid and Caldecort. Chronic usage rarely gives relief to those with pruritus. Prolonged local treatment for pruritus will not cure the condition. Proper treatment must be directed to correcting the digestive problems responsible for the pruritus, i.e., avoiding the particular sugars responsible for lactic acid formation.

Post–Colostomy Colitis

Hopefully, in the future, few will need to have their colons removed. Prior to the Colitis Club Diet, complications of severe colon disease have been treated by surgical removal of the colon and the establishment of an intestinal opening in the abdominal wall (colostomy). This procedure generally helps those with ulcerative colitis. It rarely gives lasting relief to Crohn's victims. The individual is condemned to having to wear a bag on the colostomy and suffer the inconvenience associated with it. The gas, cramping pains and profuse liquid stools may persist after the colostomy is completed, if the person is fructose or lactose intolerant.

Removing the colon and diverting the food stream away from the colon by establishing a colostomy *does not correct* intolerance to fructose, lactose, sorbitol or mannitol. If these sugars remain in the diet, the irritable bowel condition will likely persist. Even those with colostomies will improve by avoiding these sugars they cannot absorb; whether it be lactose, fructose, sorbitol, or mannitol. These sugars should be avoided by all those having irritable bowel problems, whether they have colostomies or not.

A trial on the colitis diet would be prudent for anyone facing the prospects of a colectomy or colostomy. The diet is spartan, but it is far preferable to live with a restricted diet than to live with a colostomy.

Diverticulosis

Diverticuli are small out–pouchings from the walls of the colon. They are present on the colons of nearly half of all persons over age 50. Their occurrence has been blamed on low fiber diets, as it has been observed that people in underdeveloped countries do not form diverticuli. Our studies suggest a more likely reason for the evolution of diverticulosis. In the diets of western cultures, milk and sugars make up large components of the foods consumed. In under developed countries, these foods are conspicuously absent.

As discussed elsewhere in this book, the sugars in milk, fruits and food made with corn sweetener are not fully assimilated by many people. These unabsorbed sugars ferment in the lower colon forming large volumes of gas. In western culture societies, social customs forbid the free public discharge of this gas. Irritation of the bowel wall by alcohol and lactic acid cause spasms of the bowel causing very high pressures to develop in the entrapped gas. The retained accumulations of this gas exert this pressure against the bowel. It is this gas under pressure that finds the weak spots of the bowel wall. These spots are around the blood vessels penetrating the muscle layers. Through these weak spots, the pressurized gas forces small blow outs or diverticuli to form.

For the most part, diverticuli are harmless but, occasionally, a nut or grain of popcorn plugs the opening between the diverticulum pouch and the bowel interior. When this happens, the glands lining the diverticulum produce mucus in which bacteria begin multiplying. The mucus becomes pus. Accumulation of pus in a diverticulum is called diverticulitis. With this, pressure mounts in the diverticulum and the victim presents with what appears to be left–sided appendicitis. There is pain and tenderness in the lower left side of the abdomen. Chills, fever and malaise follow. In most instances, the diverticular abscess will break back into the colon. Then after one or two foul bowel movements, normal health returns. Occasionally, diverticular abscesses break into the abdominal cavity, resulting in life–threatening peritonitis, or they may form a sinus or passage between the colon and the urinary bladder or vagina, in which case, stool will be passed in the urine or via the vagina.

Antibiotics and pain medications are helpful during the acute illness of diverticulitis. It is important to be under the observation and care of a physician during this potentially disastrous illness.

Treating irritable bowel disease with proper dietary observance will do much to prevent diverticulosis and diverticulitis.

DIVERTICULOSIS

When I get too full of gas. . . .

Spasms cause "blowouts" in my weaker areas.

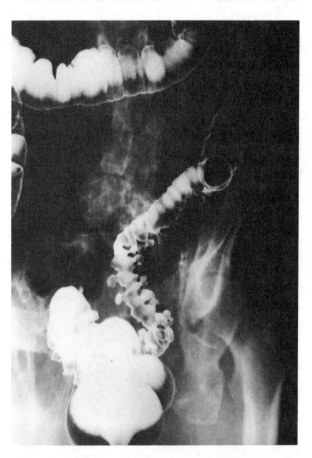

DIVERTICULOSIS The numerous cherrylike projections from the barium-filled colon are the diverticuli. These small out pouchings are caused by the gas formed by fermentation of undigested food.

Bowel Infections

Chronic infections of the digestive system may closely mimic irritable bowel syndrome. Most acute bacterial and viral infections produce symptoms of pain, diarrhea, weakness, fever, etc., that are very much like acute exacerbations of ulcerative colitis or Crohn's disease. Irritable bowel disease caused by bacterial infections tends to be short-lived. Most often, they begin rather suddenly, causing a severe illness that remits in one to seven days. Even cholera and typhoid are self-limiting in healthy individuals.

Infections of the bowel by the protozoans (one-celled animal parasites) tend to be chronic, often lasting for years. These germs of the amoeba family cause symptoms identical to those of irritable bowel disease caused by sugar intolerance. Protozoans usually come from eating or drinking contaminated food or water. Because the symptoms are the same, it is prudent for those with irritable bowel disease to have stool studies for parasites, and an eosinophile count. (This family of white blood cells increases in response to parasitic infestations.) These microbes are also communicated between homosexual men. Once rare in this country, these pathogens have become fairly common due to this new reservoir of infected persons.

Giardia lamblia is perhaps the most common protozoan parasite in this country. It is most often contracted by hunters and campers who drink water from creeks without boiling it. This tiny animal produces an illness that is clinically indistinguishable from irritable bowel syndrome. It is sometimes difficult to diagnose, requiring small bowel biopsy (see discussion on celiac sprue).

The other important protozoans, *Entamoeba histolytica, Entamoeba coli* and *Balantidium coli* are responsible for amebic dysentery. These are diagnosed by examinations of the stool, and are suspected when the eosinophile count is elevated. The Colitis Club diet will help these conditions but will not eliminate them.

Strangers Within You

Myriads of tiny plants and animals normally inhabit human colons. They are scavengers, they eat up the food nutrients which have not been assimilated in the digestive processes sort of like cats and dogs that lick up the scraps from the table. From wasted food, these organisms provide heat, and manufacture vitamins including vitamin K, essential to the body for blood clotting.

Among these miniature inhabitants are many species of bacteria. These include *E. coli*, the bacteroides family, *Streptococcus fecalis*, and *lactobacilli*. Most people harbor all of these and many, many more varieties. A number of molds and yeasts also grow in the colon including *Candida albicans*.

Bean Bugaboo

The problems beans are likely to cause colitics may go beyond the socially embarrassing production of intestinal gas. (Gas production by any food raises the suspicion flag that it may be irritating to the sensitive gastrointestinal tract.)

Most beans contain an enzyme that blocks the digestion of starches by amylase. (This blocker enzyme was briefly marketed a few years ago as a weight control aid.) The action of this substance permits starches to pass undigested into the lower intestine where bacteria ferment them. In addition to the gas, the fermentation yields irritating chemicals including alcohol, lactic acid, acetic, propionic and buteric acids.

The amount of gas formed by beans is inversely proportional to how much they are cooked. Very thorough cooking destroys the starch blocker. Lightly cooked beans are likely to contain starch blocker and cause much gas to be produced and some irritation to the bowel.

Intestinal Gases

There are only a few sources of intestinal gases. One source is swallowed air. Some swallow air unconsciously while eating or chewing gum. Others do it to induce belching for temporary relief of stomach discomfort. Much of the swallowed air is absorbed into the blood and escapes through the lungs. Some gas is formed as carbonates and reaches the stomach. Here the hydrochloric acid changes carbonates to carbon dioxide gas. Large volumes of carbon dioxide will cause burping. Smaller amounts will be absorbed into the blood and carried to the lungs for excretion.

Most of the lower intestinal gas is formed by fermentation of food stuffs in the bowel. The particular gases formed depend on which bacteria are acting on the available food substrates reaching the bowel. Social decorum mandates that this gas not be discharged in the presence of others. As we retain intestinal gas, particularly in an irritated bowel, very high pressures build. These gases are important for two reasons. They are unpleasant, and the gas confined in the irritated cramping bowel causes small herniations or diverticuli in the walls of the colon.

Carbon Dioxide

The intestinal gas formed in greatest quantity is carbon dioxide. It is formed when fats, proteins or carbohydrates are fermented. This gas readily dissolves in the blood and is carried to the lungs where it is excreted. This gas is a harmless waste produced by burning foods. Carbon dioxide is compressed into water to make carbonated water. Some decry carbonated beverages, but if one were to begin to make synthetic blood, he would start with water, then carbonate it.

Ammonia and Hydrogen Sulfide

When there is failure of the intestine to digest and absorb lactose or fructose, the resulting irritation of the bowel also impairs protein digestion and absorption. The unabsorbed protein is made available for bacterial fermentation. Fermentation of protein releases ammonia. Chemically, the amino acids that make up proteins are short carbohydrate chains with an ammonia group attached. (Ammonia is the compound resulting when one nitrogen and three hydrogen atoms combine.) Burning amino acids releases the ammonia radical; the remaining carbohydrate portion is then burned to water and carbon dioxide. Much of the ammonia produced by fermentation is absorbed into the blood where it is converted into urea. The urea is then excreted via the kidneys. Some of the ammonia may be passed as flatus (the ammonia contributing to the unpleasant odor). Some of the amino acids in protein also contain sulfur. When sulfur–containing amino acids are fermented, hydrogen sulfide or rotten egg gas is produced. This gas imparts a most disgusting odor to the flatus.

Methane and Hydrogen

Methane and hydrogen complete the list of important gases produced by colonic fermentation. Only small amounts of these gases diffuse into the blood to be excreted through the lungs. Most is passed as flatus, as these gases are insoluble in water or blood. The gases are related to fuel natural gas, and are highly combustible. One perverse form of recreation young men have been known to engage in is the lighting of matches to one another's flatus passages. This produces a mini-explosion. A few patients have been seriously injured in the course of bowel examinations: when electro-cautery is used through a colonoscope to destroy a polyp, the spark may ignite a collection of methane/hydrogen gas which then explodes.

Gallstones

Our surveys showed a close relationship between gallstones and the irritable bowel diseases. In the past, gallstones have been attributed to low fiber diets, high fat
diets, white bread and refined sugars. It is true that
gallbladder disease is very rare in under-developed
countries where refined food is not eaten. The high fiber
content of the diets in most of these countries may play
a role. However, evidence is now pointing to the failure
to assimilate the lactose and fructose in the diets of
western cultures as a more important cause. Surgeons
characterize those most prone to gallbladder disease by
listing their six Fs: Fair, Forty, Female, Fertile, Fat
and Flatulent (gassy). All of these listed factors are as
descriptive of irritable bowel disease as they are pre-
dictive of gallbladder disease.

One population in which gallstones are extremely
prevalent is the American Indian. Important clues
about why gallstones form may be learned from them.
Besides having gallbladder problems, lactose intolerance is nearly universal among adult Native Americans. They are also addicted to sweets. In modern times,
Indian people have had access to foods containing lactose and fructose. Many overindulge in soda pop, candy,
pastries and ice cream. From the author's personal observations, the average Navaho Indian's diet is a nutritional disaster. In many of the white man's foods there
is an overabundance of corn sweetener and lactose. Fail-
ing to digest these sugars results in their fermentation.
The lactic acid resulting from this fermentation
changes the acidity of the bowel contents. With the acid-

ification of the digestive stream, many insoluble elements which would ordinarily be excreted in the stool dissolve and become available for absorption. One example of this is the excessive absorption of calcium by irritable bowel victims. The increased absorption of calcium favors conditions responsible for kidney stone formation.

In a similar fashion, bile acids which are excreted from the liver and gallbladder into the intestine may be excessively reabsorbed. Normally some of the bile acid combines with calcium in the intestines to form insoluble soap. When the fecal stream is neutral or alkaline, this insoluble combination is passed out in the stool. In an acidic milieu, the calcium and the bile acid dissociate and become soluble, and both are then absorbed. The calcium is carried to the kidneys where it may make stones. The bile acid is returned to the liver to be re-excreted in the bile. In irritable bowel disease, bile acids are excreted and repeatedly reabsorbed; they cannot be discarded. This reabsorption re-excretion of bile acid results in bile that is highly concentrated with bile acid. In the gallbladder, water is removed from the bile produced by the liver. The thick super concentrated bile tends to separate and form stones in the gallbladder.

Bile acids are the body's principal means of disposing of cholesterol. Factors facilitating the excretion of bile acids such as fiber, calcium and alkaline intestinal stream help to reduce cholesterol. However, factors such as fecal acidity interfere with cholesterol excretion. This process has important implications for the health of the cardiovascular system. Irritable bowel disease reduces cholesterol excretion which results in accumulation of cholesterol in the blood and liver. High cholesterol levels contribute to atherosclerosis.

The conditions that lead to excessive bile acid reabsorption also cause excessive fatty acid absorption. The excessive fat absorption makes obesity an inescapable fact of life for many unfortunate irritable bowel owners.

Constipation

As many people with irritable bowel syndrome complain of constipation as of diarrhea. Many complain of alternating between the two. Irritation of the bowel causes both!

Passive Constipation

Constipation is usually thought of as being due to a sluggish, lazy bowel that does not move things along. This form of constipation is a passive inertia condition where waste just piles up. This is undoubtedly the cause of constipation for many. In irritable bowel disease, however, the irritated bowel tends to be hyperactive much of the time. It may move the food stream along too rapidly, causing diarrhea.

Dynamic Constipation

In normal bowel action, the muscles of the bowel contract and relax in wave like motions which move the food stream through the intestine. With irritation of the bowel lining, the bowel may become spastic. With the bowel in spasm, all of its muscles are contracted and a dynamic constipation occurs. The wave action cannot take place with all of the bowel muscles contracted. Dynamic, or spastic paralysis is as constipating as passive paralysis. But the treatment for the two is not the same. It is true that taking laxatives works in both instances, but in the case of active paralysis, the best treatment is relief of the irritation. Many laxatives tend to further irritate the bowel. In dynamic constipation, the cramps or spasms of the intestine may be very uncomfortable. By and by, segments of the colon begin to relax and contract, perhaps hyperactively again, causing loose stools. Some irritable bowel victims never know constipation as they have diarrhea continually. Others with predominently spastic colon may know only constipation. Many experience both.

Drug-Induced Colitis

Many people experience their first bouts of colitis following a course of antibiotics, especially after taking erythromycin or Cleocin. These drugs kill many normal bowel inhabitants, but spare, and seem to facilitate, the growth of a bacteria called *Clostridium difficile*. This bacteria is a cousin to the tetanus and botulism organisms. It produces a toxin that damages the bowel wall, producing a condition called pseudomembranous colitis, a severe prolonged irritable bowel ailment. This results in the loss of the enzymes necessary to digest lactose and fructose. This irritable bowel condition is self-perpetuating. It interferes with the digestion of not only

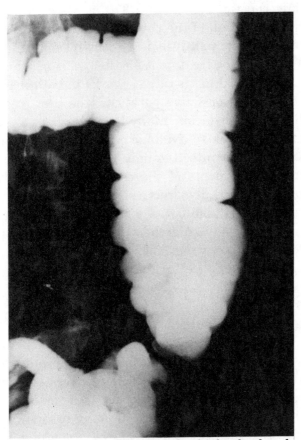

PASSIVE CONSTIPATION Most people think of a lax, lazy, dilated colon in association with constipation. This is common in nursing home patients who spend most of their time in bed. The active constipation is of more interest to those with irritable bowel disease.

SPASTIC CONSTIPATION Most common but seldom appreciated is spastic constipation. The movement of the food stream through the intestine depends on the coordinated rhythmic contractions of the two layers of muscle in the intestinal wall. A caustic stream irritates the bowel causing spasm as shown above. Nothing moves through this bowel, and discomfort may range from unnoticeable to very painful.

lactose and fructose, but also other foodstuffs which ferment and cause further irritation. The colitis diet is the best means of correcting the problem. By avoiding the irritating sugars, the bowel lining is allowed to heal. In time, tolerance to these sugars improves, though there may be some persistent intolerance.

Bowel lining injury by antibiotics (or other drugs) is one of the most common ways irritable bowel disease begins. Many individuals I have treated were unaware of any symptoms of food intolerance until they were given antibiotics such as ampicillin or erythromycin by their doctors. When antibiotics cause colitis, it is time for immediate medical intervention. Probably the antibiotic will have to be stopped and cortisone taken for one or two days. The colitis diet should then be used until normalcy returns.

Drug-induced colitis may follow many drugs, including diuretics, those for high blood pressure, and anti-diabetes pills. Any of the antibiotics can be irritating to the bowel, causing colitis.

Radiation Colitis

Colitis often follows radiation therapy for cancer. Radiation injures, often permanently, the delicate bowel lining. As the mucosa is damaged, there is a reduction in the amount of digestive enzymes produced. As a result, many foods fail to digest and are passed into the lower digestive tract undigested. Fermentation follows and a vicious cycle of maldigestion—malabsorption—fermentation—bowel irritation—maldigestion, etc., is established. Prominent among the foods that fail to digest are the sugars. Most post-radiation colitis victims will note improvement on the Colitis Club Diet. After allowing a few months for the bowel to repair itself, tolerance of these sugars may improve.

The Colitis-Arthritis Connection

For some time, it has been recognized that one of the complications of the irritable bowel disease is arthritis. As the reports came in from our survey, many victims of colitis experienced improvement of their arthritis when they treated their colitis with the research diet. This suggested that the arthritis many people suffer is due to colitis or irritable bowel syndrome. The significance of this is that for many, the correct treatment of their arthritis is not drugs but diet.

When the colitis research questionnaire was first drawn up, it was used to survey members of a celiac sprue convention. When these questionnaires were tabulated, some surprising associations were noted. One fifth of the celiac sprue victims had had kidney stones. One half of the respondents also suffered from arthritis! The high frequency of kidney stones among the celiac sprue victims prompted the question: Might not individuals with kidney stones show a high frequency of irritable bowel disease?

The same questionnaire was sent out to the Kidney Stone Formers Club membership. As the results of this second survey came in, it was apparent that at least half of the kidney stone formers had irritable bowel disease which was responsible for the formation of their kidney stones. Half of the kidney stone formers also had arthritis! The high association of arthritis and irritable bowel disease prompted another question: Might not the arthritis be due to irritable bowel disease? The results from the colitis survey indicated that 50 percent of those with colitis and arthritis experienced improvement in their arthritis as the colitis improved. This preliminary evidence suggests that a high percentage of victims of arthritis have this disease as a consequence of irritable bowel disease.

Cholesterol Message for Colitics

In the 1950s, simple chemical analysis of the waxy material in arteriosclerotic plaques of diseased arteries yielded cholesterol. Since then cholesterol has been a dirty word. People were cautioned not to eat eggs as they contained cholesterol. Then for 30 years, eggs has also been a dirty word. (See Appendix: Navaho Indians Don't Get Cancer.)

Cholesterol is a wax that closely resembles paraffin.* I have been baffled and perplexed at the readiness of the medical profession and the public to accept the idea that cholesterol is absorbed from the diet into the blood. This substance simply will not dissolve in water. Be-

---

*Chocolate candy is made by mixing chocolate and sugar in paraffin wax. This is regarded as safe, because the paraffin wax is not absorbable.

cause of this, I have secretly been a closet doubter regarding the theories that cholesterol in the diet played any significant role in human disease or nutrition. In recent years (in very tiny print), the medical establishment confessed they could not trace labeled cholesterol from eggs into the human bloodstream. Instead, the body manufactures cholesterol. Cholesterol is an essential constituent of the brain. It is also the chassis or chemical frame the sex hormones and cortisone are built on.

(In the late 1960s, a chemical was marketed that blocked cholesterol production. It was sold under the name MER-29. After two years, many of those taking the drug suffered degeneration of the brain!)

The body excretes cholesterol in the bile as cholic acid. It is secreted as the sodium or potassium salts (soaps). These substances are soluble in water and act as detergents in spreading the digestive juices throughout the food stream. In colitics, these salts tend to be excessively reabsorbed as evidenced by the high rate of gallstone formation. After reabsorption, they are removed from the blood by the liver and re-excreted in the bile. This repeated absorption and excretion overloads the biliary system by putting excessive bile salt in the available biliary fluid. Precipitation takes place in the super–saturated bile and cholesterol biliary stones form.

Cholic acid reabsorption can be blocked with calcium supplements. Calcium combines with the cholic acid and forms an insoluble soap that passes in the stool. (A recent study reported the lowering of blood cholesterol with calcium supplements. Removing excess cholic acid is the probable mechanism.) One study is now underway to confirm this report. Calcium supplements and the treatment of IBD may soon prove to be the best way to prevent atherosclerosis.

Potassium for Colitics

Many individuals with irritable bowel disease are older and are taking diuretics for hypertension or heart failure. Persons taking these drugs are cautioned that the medications may cause excessive loss of potassium. Body potassium levels are critical for the heart. Either too much or too little can cause serious rhythm irregularities that may be fatal. The higher the diuretic dosage, the more potassium will be lost, and the more crucial it is to replace it with supplements or to take agents to prevent its loss. To counter these losses, patients are advised to increase their potassium intake by drinking orange juice and eating bananas. With both of these foods on the colitis diet forbidden list, what are irritable bowel sufferers who take diuretics to do?

In this respect, the colitis diet is quite restrictive, but there are alternatives. Baked potatoes have amounts of potassium comparable to oranges and bananas. (Don't boil them—boiling leaches out the potassium.) Tomatoes are also equally rich in this element, as are meat, fish and poultry.

Most individuals on diuretics are given potassium supplements which adequately protect their reserves. Those on supplements need not be greatly concerned about dietary supplementation. Some diuretics such as Dyazide and Maxide contain triamterene, which prevents potassium loss from the kidneys. This usually makes supplementation with diet or pills unnecessary. Some doctors prescribe spironolactone, or Aldactone with the thiazide diuretics. This more powerful agent causes sodium (salt) to be excreted and potassium to be retained. Potassium supplements are not to be taken with this drug as it poses the opposite danger—that of excessively high potassium levels, a peril as grave as a potassium level that is too low.

Vitamin C

Many write to the Colitis Club expressing concern that they may not be getting enough vitamin C if they stop eating fruits. The Colitis Diet sharply limits the amount of fructose one eats. In doing this, all sweet fruits must be avoided. There are other foods which are allowed, however, that contain significant amounts of this vitamin, such as fresh tomatoes, fresh cabbage, and most other fresh vegetables (cooking destroys vitamin C).

For many, it may be desirable to take a vitamin supplement that contains a substantial amount of vitamin C. Those with irritable bowel disease will do well to learn to love meat and vegetables.

Colitis-Alzheimer's Connection?

The irritable bowel disease may greatly predispose one to Alzheimer's disease. So far, there have been no detailed studies, but on theoretical grounds, these diseases put one at much greater risk. The acidification of the digestive system that occurs in irritable bowel disease increases the amount of some metals that will be absorbed. For example, the acidic bowel absorbs too much calcium and kidney stones result. This same acidification facilitates the absorption of lead, mercury, cadmium, tin, zinc and aluminum.

Several recent studies point an incriminating finger at aluminum as a possible cause of neurologic diseases such as Alzheimer's. Evidence for this comes from several fronts. Alzheimer's–like symptoms have been induced in cats, rabbits, monkeys, rats and mice by giving them toxic amounts of aluminum. Memory, learning and behavioral changes were observed in the test animals. It was noted that younger animals were more resistant to aluminum intoxication than were older animals. The filaments of the brain cells of the aluminum–treated animals showed tangles that resemble those observed in the brain tissues of Alzheimer's victims.

Some individuals undergoing dialysis for kidney failure develop an Alzheimer's–like dementia. Ted L. Petit, Ph.D., of the Division of Life Sciences, University of Toronto, Canada, reported in *The American Journal of Kidney Diseases*: "Aluminum has been strongly implicated in human dialysis dementia. This syndrome is characterized by speech difficulties, motor abnormalities, personality changes, seizures, and progressive dementia terminating in convulsions and death. The syndrome is remarkably similar to the syndrome previously described in both experimental animals and non-diseased humans exposed to elevated levels of aluminum. A number of studies have shown that particularly in the brain, aluminum is elevated in patients with dialysis dementia. A number of researchers have shown that dialysis dementia is associated with high aluminum content in the water used to make up the dialysate, and when deionized water is substituted, an elimination or reduction of dementia is observed."

According to another authority, Zaven S. Khachaturian, Ph.D., from the Physiology of Aging Branch, National Institute on Aging, of the National Institutes of Health, the Chamorros natives of Guam ". . . have a remarkably high incidence of such neuro-degenerative disorders as amyotrophic lateral sclerosis and Parkinson-dementia-lateral sclerosis complex, have high levels of aluminum in their brains." In Guam, this condition accounts for 15 percent of all adult deaths. Non–natives living in Guam for more than 20 years suffer the same fate.

Dr. Daniel Perl, of the Department of Pathology of the University of Vermont College of Medicine, used a highly sensitive scanning electron microscope in conjunction with spectrometry apparatus and identified abnormal accumulations of aluminum within neurons (nerve cells) derived from patients with Alzheimer's disease.

Aluminum is the most abundant metallic element in the earth's crust, comprising about five percent. In rocks and compounds in which it occurs in nature, however, it is extremely insoluble and has been biologically unavailable until man learned to refine it into its metallic state. Most of the aluminum absorption appears to come from refined metallic sources. More investigation into this relationship is going on. Further developments on this subject will be forthcoming.

Common sources of aluminum are cooking pots and pans, some antacids and aluminum soda pop cans. Prevention of the absorption of aluminum and other undesirable metals depends on the treatment of the irritable bowel disease with appropriate dietary measures, avoidance of aluminum food containers and making the dietary stream more alkaline by flooding the bowel with supplementary calcium.

Cancer of the Colon

Irritable bowel disease greatly predisposes one to cancer of the colon. Each year, 2 ½ percent of those with ulcerative colitis develop cancer. That may not sound like many, but it amounts to 25 percent each ten years and 50 percent every 20 years! This alone makes it imperative to treat bowel conditions in the very best manner and to initiate a surveillance plan to detect cancer as early as possible. Following the dietary guidelines of this book will reduce the inflammation of the bowel lining, thereby reducing its susceptibility to cancer.

There are a number of theories as to why bowel cancer develops. One is that bile acids irritate the intestinal wall when there is slow transit of the food stream. Another is that lack of fiber in the diet results in the early death of fecal bacteria. This releases a toxin, fecapentaene, from the bacterial bodies that cause it.

The author happens to subscribe to the germ theory of disease: that cancer of the bowel results from the invasion of the bowel lining where it is broken by chronic irritation, by any of a number of known cancer-causing viruses that abound in the foods we eat from the animal world. Irritation by those elements responsible for irritable bowel syndrome allow these carcinogenic viruses, present in a number of our foods, to colonize and start a tumor. These viruses come from animal foods that have not been sufficiently cooked to destroy all of the germs that are present. Virtually all the cancers occurring in the animal kingdom are traced to these viruses.

Many people insist on eating meat that is not thoroughly cooked. What they fail to realize (perhaps no one ever told them) is that between 20 and 30 percent of all cattle are infected with bovine leukemia virus. This virus is closely related to the AIDS agent. It causes cancer in the cattle. Eating rare meat often involves the consumption of this virus in an infective state!

A like percentage of the dairy cows in the country are infected with leukemia virus. These animals shed it in their milk. Since one third of the cows harbor this agent, all of the commercial milk is contaminated. At least one study has suggested that pasteurization does not eradicate the virus from commercial milk.

Other sources of cancer–causing viruses are eggs and chickens. Since no one eats rare chicken, consumption of cooked chicken poses little or no danger. The eating of raw eggs (as in eggnog or Caesar salad) is very dangerous. Also dangerous is the eating of soft or over easy eggs. These eggs are not heated sufficiently to kill the leukosis and Marek's viruses that cause cancer in the chickens. One reason chicken is inexpensive to buy is that laying hens are butchered when they are two years old, not because they have stopped laying (they are in the prime of their egg laying careers), but because they begin dying of cancer! The author recalls personally butchering hens with three different kinds of cancer.

To avoid bowel and most other common cancers maintain a healthy bowel lining and cook meat, eggs and milk thoroughly. For more evidence supporting this concept, refer to the Appendix: Navaho Indians Do Not Get Cancer.

Cancer Surveillance

Checking the stool for occult blood is important for all people in order to detect cancers of the bowel as early as possible. This is doubly important for those with irritable bowel disease. If there is a common denominator among those who get bowel cancer, it is irritable bowel disease.

Cancers are disorganized tissues that invade blood vessels and cause them to leak. The simplest means of detecting bowel cancers is to test the stool for traces of blood. There are several good home tests for this purpose. Hemoccult, Fleet Detecatest, CS-T Colo Screen Self Test, are a few. Hemoccult and Fleet Detecatest require the smearing of a small quantity of stool on a paper and applying a drop of peroxide; the presence of blood is indicated by a purple color. CS-T Colo Screen requires only the floating of a special tissue on the water in the commode to detect blood. The merits of these tests can be debated. It is more important to do any of them than to be concerned over which is best. It is important to stop taking vitamin C three days before doing these tests, as vitamin C will cause a false negative test. Some foods such as turnips and radishes may also interfere.

Any visible blood in the stool should be investigated. The American Cancer Society advises an inspection of the inside of the bowel by proctoscopy annually. In view of their increased risk, this is especially good advice for victims of irritable bowel disease. There are several causes of blood in the stool other than cancer. Hemorrhoids often rupture and leave bright red blood on the toilet tissue. Large hard stools may tear the lining of the rectum, again leaving stains on the tissue. Bleeding is a common occurrence with more severe ulcerative colitis. Diverticulosis often causes bleeding that, at times, may be massive. The stalks of polyps, mole–like growths from the bowel wall, may tear causing bleeding. Polyps are important as it is generally believed that cancer most often begins on the ends of these growths. A positive test is not reason for despair, but it is the signal to get help as soon as possible.

Examinations of the Colon

There are two means of examining the interior of the bowel: Barium enema x-rays and direct inspection with a proctoscope or colonoscope. The barium enema involves the flowing of liquid barium sulfate into the colon and recording its shadows on x-ray film. Generally, the flow of the barium is observed by the radiologist with a fluoroscopic plate or an image intensifier. X-ray plates are exposed periodically. The procedure is usually followed by air contrast studies. After the colon is filled with barium and the x-rays exposed, the barium is evacuated from the bowel. A thin layer of barium adheres to the bowel wall. The colon is then inflated with air. Many details obscured by the barium enema then become apparent.

The colonoscopic examination is made usually with a flexible telescope which is inserted into the colon. Examinations are made of the lining for various distances into the colon. This procedure is particularly helpful in the lower colon where spine and pelvis shadows may obscure the x-ray details of the bowel. These examinations are complementary; both are important.

Fiber for Colitics

Stemming from Dr. Burkitt's observations that the high fiber eating African natives rarely get bowel cancer, gallstones, appendicitis, hemorrhoids or many other common gastrointestinal ailments, there has been a great increase in interest in dietary fiber. He attributed this lack of gastrointestinal ills to the fiber in their diets. The shelves of bookstores are crammed with diet books by self-styled authorities, most of whom are on the fiber bandwagon. All kinds of great and wonderful things are touted by these fiber advocates. However, one must be careful in assigning explanations for observations such as the absence of bowel cancer among African natives.

The observation that these people do not get gastrointestinal diseases is probably valid. That fiber is the primary element responsible is debatable and doubtful. It is equally true that these same diets are low in lactose and fructose. The absence of these sugars accounts equally well for the rarity of intestinal problems. While fiber may be protective, it is just as likely that the absence of bowel cancer is due to the absence of these sugars or animal proteins in their diets.

Contrary to current medical advice, fiber and wheat bran are *not* good for irritable bowels. Fiber is composed of complex carbohydrates that are poorly digested. In many people, poorly digested fiber causes the very same problems that the poorly digested sugars do: it ferments and produces gas, cramping and diarrhea!

In one study, it was found that rats fed on a wheat bran diet had significant intestinal bleeding! Wheat is the cause of colitis in celiac sprue victims. (Their symptoms are indistinguishable from those who have colitis due to lactose or fructose intolerance. There is a considerable crossing–over effect, i.e., celiac victims who are intolerant of wheat are often intolerant of lactose and fructose as well. Lactose or fructose intolerant individuals may have poor tolerance of wheat bran—particularly in large amounts.)

In spite of all the bad things said about refined foods, they have a certain beauty about them for persons with irritable bowel diseases. Cane sugar, white bread and potatoes are all converted into glucose and absorbed into the blood quite completely. This leaves little residue to pass into the lower digestive tract to ferment. (One study indicated that mashed potatoes raised blood glucose levels almost as quickly as sugar itself. This showed that the conversion of potato starch to glucose and its absorption takes place very rapidly.)

The fermentation and gas-producing qualities of

beans, cabbage and many other foods are inversely related to how long they are cooked. The more they are
cooked (a refining process that partially digests foods by
breaking down the complex carbohydrates into simple
sugars), the less they ferment and produce gas and irritating chemicals.

If fiber causes you to have colitis symptoms, it is
best to avoid it. Brown bread is perhaps a little more
nutritious than white, but if it causes bowel irritation,
then white bread is far better for you. Do not feel you
must obey all the rules of all the experts, including this
one. Find what works for you. This volume is to be used
as a guide for a rational approach to finding the foods
responsible for your irritable bowel disease.

IBS as a Cause of Kidney Stones

Stone formation in the urinary tract (renal lithiasis) has
been recognized as a frequent complication of ulcerative
colitis and Crohn's disease. This association prompted
a survey of the kidney stone formers to determine the
converse situation. How frequently do the irritable bowel
diseases occur among stone formers? Analysis of 498
survey questionnaires suggested that at least 50 percent
of kidney stone formers have symptoms indicative of
irritable bowel disease. This survey also suggested that
many of these stone formers make their stones because
of faulty digestion rather than faulty kidneys. Irritable
bowel patients are all at risk for forming kidney stones
because the acidic intestinal milieu allows too much cal-

cium to be absorbed. The kidneys may not be able to handle the excess calcium.

In the autumn of 1985, survey questionnaires were mailed out to the 1,500 members of the Kidney Stone Formers Club. This organization was sponsored by *The Saturday Evening Post*. This study is based on the 498 questionnaires returned by the club members:

	Yes Answers
Questions in the survey included:	
1. Have you ever been diagnosed as having ulcerative colitis?	13
2. Do you have Crohn's disease?	8
3. Do you have "spastic colitis"?	39
4. Do you have celiac sprue?	3
5. Do you have frequent bouts of diarrhea?	90
6. Do you have cramping abdominal pains?	95
7. Do you make excessive intestinal gas?	200
8. Do you have frequent bouts of constipation?	69
9. Do you have food intolerances?	105
10. Do you have lactose (milk sugar) intolerance?	45
11. Do you make intestinal gas after eating milk or ice cream?	93
12. Do you have pruritus (rectal itching) after milk or ice cream?	13
13. Do you have fructose (fruit sugar) intolerance?	18
14. Does orange juice cause gas or diarrhea?	69
15. Do bananas or apples cause gas or diarrhea?	80
16. Do you get pruritus after eating fruit?	15
17. Does candy cause gas or diarrhea?	31
18. Have you had hemorrhoids?	245
19. Have you had arthritis?	163
20. Have you had skin problems?	145

21. Have you had eczema?   59
22. Have you had psoriasis?   30
23. Have you had gallstones?   69

The high incidence of gastrointestinal symptoms in kidney stone formers is striking. Intestinal gas production, frequent bouts of diarrhea, abdominal cramping pains, food intolerances point to a high incidence of irritable bowel disease among kidney stone formers. Two hundred of the respondents indicated they had excessive intestinal gas production, 90 had frequent bouts of diarrhea and 95 reported abdominal cramping pains. The high frequency of these symptoms indicates that irritable bowel disease is extremely common among stone formers, but often has not been diagnosed as such.

Question number 10 indicates how many have been diagnosed as having lactose intolerance while the number who get irritable bowel symptoms from ice cream (high in both lactose and fructose) is twice as great. Only 18 were aware of fructose intolerance but at least 80 either made gas or experienced diarrhea from orange juice, apples or bananas. The recognized kidney stone formation in Crohn's and ulcerative colitis, and the above frequent association of irritable bowel disease and renal lithiasis suggests a common mechanism for the formation of kidney stones which has not been fully appreciated.

The failure to metabolize lactose has been acknowledged as a common cause of irritable bowel symptoms. Not previously recognized is a syndrome nearly identical to lactose intolerance, but due to fructose intolerance. When these sugars are not digested and absorbed, they reach the lower digestive tract where their fermentation produces gases, alcohol and lactic acid. Besides being highly irritating to the bowel mucosa, the acid lowers the pH of the fecal stream. As the bowel contents become more acidic, many calcium salts—such as calcium carbonate, the calcium salts of the bile acids, calcium phosphate, etc.—that are insoluble in neutral or alkaline milieus become soluble. Lowering the pH by even small increments greatly increases the amount of calcium available for absorption into the bloodstream. The excess blood calcium is then presented to the kidneys for excretion. The increased calcium excretion load causes supersaturation of the urine and stone formation results. The kidneys, far from being culprits in stone formation, are the victims of excessive calcium absorption due to sugar fermentation in the gut. This appears to be a mechanism for kidney stone formation in irritable bowel syndrome as well as in ulcerative colitis and Crohn's.

This survey also noted a high incidence of gallstones (69) in kidney stone formers. This observation appears to support the concept that irritable bowel disease provoked by lactose/fructose intolerance contributes to kidney stone development. When insoluble calcium salts of bile acid are subjected to acidification, both the calcium and the bile acid radicals become available for absorption. This allows continuous reabsorption and re-excretion of bile acids causing super saturation of the bile with these compounds. Gallstone formation is the consequence. Hence, the frequent association of gallstones and kidney stones (as reflected in the series).

The surprisingly high incidence of several conditions

seemingly unrelated to kidney stones, such as hemorrhoids (245), arthritis (163), skin problems (145) and psoriasis (30), perhaps reflects a common underlying
digestive problem and further study of these associations may reveal a syndrome.

The implications of this survey suggest that, for
many stone formers, attention should be directed at correcting the problems arising from the gastrointestinal
tract rather than trying to medically manipulate conditions in the kidneys. This means avoiding lactose and/
or fructose, sorbitol and mannitol. It is important to
bear in mind that the kidneys cannot make calcium.
They are, however, burdened with the task of excreting
all the excess calcium the faulty gastrointestinal system
absorbs. In the past, we may have been looking too hard
and in the wrong places to find reasons for kidney stone
formation. We have made great efforts to find inhibiting
substances that the faulty kidneys were not making.
Lack of inhibitors does not account for hypercalciuria.
By concentrating attention on the kidneys, we perhaps
miss mildly symptomatic irritable bowel disease that
causes excess calcium absorption and plays a major role
in the development of many kidney stones.

To summarize, 498 kidney stone formers responded
to a survey questionnaire and showed a very high frequency of irritable bowel disease symptoms. This study
suggests that irritable bowel disease is a major factor
in the hyper-absorption of calcium that frequently leads
to kidney stones.

Failure to Digest Food

Food passes through the bodies of some individuals with irritable bowel problems without being digested. Digestive failure is accompanied by absorptive failure and malnutrition.

Too rapid transit of the food may prevent the digestive enzymes from acting on it. More often, the pancreas is not producing adequate pancreatic lipases (to digest fats), amylase (to digest starch) and proteases (to digest proteins). (The failure of the bowel mucosa to produce lactase and fructose aldolase is the hallmark of irritable bowel disease.) The treatment of irritable bowel disease is to reduce consumption of these sugars for which enzymes are lacking.

Enzyme Replacement

Treatment for pancreatic insufficiency is the replacement of these enzymes. Happily, the beauty of enzyme replacements is their safety. You could eat a truckload of them with no ill effects. Replacement enzymes include Cotazyme, Festalan, Gustase, Kutrase, Ku-Zyme and Pancreatin. These are safe to try with any of the irritable bowel conditions.

The lack of digestive enzymes for specific food elements is the basis for most irritable bowel diseases. As has been pointed out, lack of enzymatic competence for changing fructose to glucose is a major element. Insufficiency of other enzymes also allows undigested foods to ferment in the intestine.

Enzymatic deficiency may be present for specific food elements but, most often, deficiencies are multiple. The cause for the deficiency of one enzyme often results in multiple deficiencies. Failure to digest (and absorb) multiple foodstuffs results in malnutrition. (Note: Taking vitamins and minerals will *not* correct protein or carbohydrate deficiencies.)

The end result of the irritable bowel diseases is malabsorption and malnutrition. The loss of the epithelial brush border with its enzyme production causes failure of foods to be digested. Foods are not broken down and consequently not absorbed. The undigested-unabsorbed foodstuffs pass into the lower digestive tract where they ferment. This produces toxic substances that irritate the bowel wall. Severe diarrhea with cramps and mucus follows, resulting in weight loss, anemia and malnutrition.

One strategy outlined in this book is the avoidance of the foods that most commonly fail digestion. Enzyme replacement therapy is a second option for those with malnutrition caused by enzymatic insufficiency. One ploy that has helped some irritable bowel sufferers is to replace the lost enzymes with plant or animal enzyme preparations. This is particularly useful in situations where a large portion of the intestine has been removed or has been injured by radiation treatments.

Health food stores supply enzyme supplements that are acceptable and usually less expensive than proprietary formulas.

One enzyme supplement has already been mentioned—the lactose replacement (Lactaid or Lactrase) to aid in the digestive process of turning lactose into glucose. (There is no comparable enzyme available to convert fructose to glucose.) The number of enzyme replacements is limited and they tend to be expensive. Most come as tablets or powders to be taken with meals or mixed in the food. The enzyme supplements are remarkably safe.

A surprising number of my patients with malabsorption get significant benefit from the kitchen enzyme preparation, meat tenderizer. They mix ½ teaspoon of Adolph's meat tenderizer with each meal. This product of papaya is an inexpensive means of replacing some digestive enzymes.

Certain foods may also be sources of these important digestive enzymes. The lactobacilli involved in making yogurt and cottage cheese produce lactase and other enzymes. They make these enzymes so they can break down lactose and other substrates for their own metabolism. The bacteria actually produce an excess of enzymes. An individual can take advantage of this excess by eating either cottage cheese or yogurt when he indulges in foods such as ice cream or fruits that contain lactose or fructose. The bacterial enzymes will digest a modest amount of these sugars when the individual may not have the enzymes to do the job alone.

Brewer's malt is rich in enzymes and may work well for some. Papayas and pineapple are other enzyme–rich foods one may try, remembering they also contain fructose.

Weight Control Problems

Of the problems perplexing irritable bowel victims, the inability to control weight is perhaps the most common and the most frustrating. Diet after diet, and miracle pill after miracle pill are vainly tried. By adhering to an extremely low-caloric diet, most can lose a few pounds—only to regain them immediately after stopping the diet. Most infuriating are the remarks from others and particularly from doctors, "You are simply eating too much." This is probably true in some instances, but most overweight IBS victims actually eat less than thin people who do not have IBS. Eating the same amount of food as a non-IBS person, the one with IBS will gain weight and become obese while the others do not. Perhaps there is an explanation.

Digestion of Fats

Fatty acids are very poorly soluble in water and are extremely weak acids. Because of their very low solubility (fatty acids would rather dissolve in organic solvents such as ether or gasoline), there is normally a heavy wastage. Much of the insoluble free fatty acid remains in the food stream and is passed in the stool.

Much of the fat consumed, particularly fats from animal sources, comes in the form of triglyceride. Three molecules of fatty acid are joined to one molecule of glycerol. The enzyme lipase splits the fatty acids away from the glycerol.

```
G—Fatty acid
L
Y
C—Fatty acid + lipase  →   glycerol + 3 fatty acids
E
R
O
L—Fatty acid
Triglyceride
```

The irritable bowel appears to absorb more of the fatty acids than is normal. The milieu in the irritable bowel either enhances the breakdown of triglycerides by lipase, or increases the absorption of the fatty acids.

Preliminary evidence suggests that large supplements of calcium will cause the free fatty acids and bile acids to form insoluble calcium soaps that will be excreted in the stool. (See "Weight Control for Colitics" in Chapter 4.) Reducing the amount of fat one absorbs will block the reaccumulation of fat lost by reducing diets.

Fatty acids are also soluble in the alcohol produced in the fermentation process. This may be another route for excessive fat absorption by colitics.

Hiatus Hernia

Hiatus hernia occurs when the esophageal opening in the diaphragm allows part of the stomach to escape from the abdomen into the chest cavity. This may come about

NORMAL

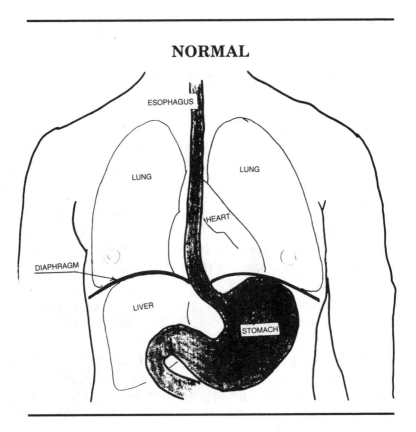

as a result of a congenitally enlarged esophageal opening in the diaphragm. Others develop this hernia from
a severe blow to the abdomen as in an auto accident or
an explosion.

In irritable bowel disease, the gaseous inflation of
the bowel compromises the available space in the abdomen. This exerts a constant pressure upward on the
stomach—forcing part of that organ into the chest.
Often these same people are obese and fat stores in

HIATUS HERNIA

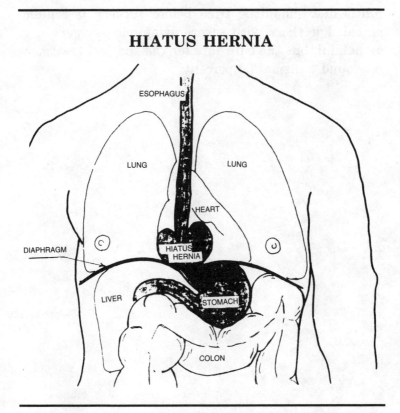

the abdomen further encroach on the available space in the abdominal cavity, adding to the pressure on the stomach.

Aging also plays a role as weakness of the diaphragm muscle allows the hiatus, or esophageal opening, to relax and enlarge. This permits some of the stomach to be pressed into the chest space between the lungs and behind the heart.

Weight reduction and anti-gas measures such as the

colitis diet should be tried before surgery is contemplated. For those with severe symptoms, surgery may be helpful, but the cure rate for the surgical treatment is around a dismal 50 percent.

Chapter 4

Dietary Considerations

Dietology

To arrive at a diet compatible with one's digestive system may require that one discard many old notions that have been accepted as fact. The very worst diet is the one that irritates the bowel—no matter what its vitamin and mineral virtues might be. The first goal is to find a diet that does not harm the intestine. Secondarily, one may worry about nutrient values; not the other way about. The irritated bowel does not absorb nutrients well and no matter how nutritious the food might be, unabsorbed nutrients are useless.

The notion that optimum health requires a quart of milk per day must be disregarded by most colitics. The idea that fiber is important to health must likewise be put aside. Fiber and complex carbohydrates often behave in the same manner that poorly digested sugars do in the irritable bowel. The undigested fiber serves as fodder for bacteria and yeasts in the colon. In irritable bowel disease, the ideal is to eat carbohydrates that are rapidly converted to glucose and quickly absorbed. Cooking food is the most practical way of "predigesting" foods so this rapid conversion to glucose can occur.

To the students of dietology, some striking similarities will be noted between the colitis diet outlined in this book and some others that are popular right now. Dr. William G. Crook's *Yeast Connection* diet avoids many carbohydrates, including fructose and lactose. The benefits noted from Dr. Crook's diet probably result from the exclusion of these sugars rather than from the program as a whole. The diet alone is probably as effective as the diet plus the antifungal drug. *The Yeast Connection* makes many unscientific propositions: One is that complex carbohydrates are good, and refined (simple) carbohydrates are bad. The prescribed diet probably does nothing to reduce yeast proliferation, as yeast grows equally well on complex carbohydrates (yeast grows quite well on sawdust or cardboard!). A second erroneous proposition is that undesirable fermentation in the gastrointestinal tract is mainly due to yeast. There are myriads of different kinds of microorganisms in the gut. In addition to yeast, many species of bacteria attack and ferment any good substrate that may be available. The anti-yeast diet also recommends the avoidance of raised bakery foods. While it is true these employ yeast for leavening, baking destroys all of the yeast organisms. In addition, the bread yeasts are quite different from the monilial yeasts discussed in his book, which grow in and on people. Bread yeast never infects humans. When bread spoils, mold—not yeast— attacks it.

The Yeast Connection diet is beneficial for some people—probably not because of its anti-yeast action but because lactose and fructose are excluded.

Another diet that has proven to be beneficial to some adherents is that of Dr. Collin H. Dong. In his book *New Hope for the Arthritic*, he recommends a diet high in protein and vegetables and the elimination of dairy products and fruit sugar. The diet professed little scientific basis. It is patterned after the Chinese diet of vegetables, pork, chicken, beef, fish and rice. (Note the absence of lactose and fructose.)

Arthritis is one of the common complications of IBS. Many people following the colitis diet have noted improvement in their arthritis. Personally I can tell an immediate aggravation of my mild arthritis upon departures from the diet when significant amounts of fructose have been consumed.

Dr. Dong's diet also avoids red meat. Meat avoidance perhaps reduces uric acid production and may help avoid gout, one cause of arthritis. I fail to see the difference between consuming red meat and poultry, as both produce purine or uric acid. I am convinced this diet helps many with their arthritis, but not for the reasons Dr. Dong says. Instead, it relieves an underlying irritable bowel condition that is causing the arthritis.

These two diets hit on some of the right combinations empirically rather than with sound chemical principles in mind. The Dong diet does recognize lactose intolerance but does not regard it as a primary item, but rather as secondary to problems from the immune system.

Weight Control for Colitics

As a young country doctor, I doubted the veracity of my many obese middle-age patients who insisted they gained weight in spite of eating very sparingly. I now recognize that this is often true. Another doubter reported in the *British Medical Journal* (292:983–987) that, contrary to expectations, obese women had higher rates of metabolism than matched thin women. This shattered the theory that the obese became fat because they did not burn calories as rapidly as lean persons. There are factors involved that appear to contradict the accepted concept of energy balance: When you expend more energy than you consume in food you lose weight, and when you eat more than you burn, you gain weight. Some gain weight while others do not when they eat the same amount of food.

As most of those who suffer from the irritable bowel have associated weight problems, some suggestions for weight control are offered here. Those with severe diarrhea suffer marked malabsorption and are underweight and malnourished. Since the food stream passes through so fast, little of the nutrients are absorbed. For these, good nutrition depends on alleviating the irritation of the intestine so it may perform its absorptive functions.

Many more individuals having less severe colitis suffer hyperabsorption of fats, bile acids, calcium, and other metals. For these, obesity is the problem. They gain weight even while eating very carefully. These victims try many weight loss programs, but none are successful. Starvation type diets allow them to lose a little weight, but it always comes back almost immediately.

Farmers have long been aware that "You cannot fatten hogs on wheat." Wheat has a high starch content and is low in fat. Corn, on the other hand, has a fairly high fat content. Thus to fatten hogs, you must provide them with preformed fat! In recent years, researchers have arrived at the same conclusion about the human body. It, too, is very poor at turning carbohydrates into fat. This observation has tremendous implications for irritable bowel sufferers. It suggests that the fat accumulated in the body is fat which has been eaten, not fat that has been manufactured in the body by the conversion of carbohydrates or proteins. You do not become fat from eating carbohydrates, but from eating fats. In mild irritable bowel disease, fats are absorbed excessively.

Bathtub Ring Chemistry

The author proposes an entirely new approach to weight control for colitis victims based on the chemistry of the bathtub ring. In hard water (rich in calcium), a scum forms on the top of the water that sticks to the sides of the tub. The bathtub ring is formed when the calcium in the water combines with the oils from the skin to form an insoluble calcium soap. It occurred to the author that intestinal absorption of fats might be reduced in this same manner. By taking calcium supplements with meals containing fat (butter, cooking oil, meat fats etc.), might not much of the fat be turned into "bathtub ring" and made insoluble in the intestine so it could not be absorbed? This concept is attractive for use by those with irritable bowel problems, as they as a group tend to absorb a much higher percentage of fats eaten than do non-colitics. For this reason, they tend to be more obese and form gallstones. Recently it was demonstrated that calcium supplements reduced cholesterol—by this same mechanism. The calcium binds the bile acids (made from cholesterol) in the intestinal tract, thus preventing reabsorption into the blood cholesterol pool.

Another study done in Germany reported that the rate of gallstone formation was not reduced by following a high fiber/low cholesterol/high polyunsaturated fat diet. This directly counters the current theories about gallstone formation. It strongly supports, however, the theory that gallstones are due to the hyper-absorption of lipids (fats) in irritable bowel disease.

The application of this concept was tried on a group of nine heavy women who had had their gallbladders removed (this told me that they were hyper-absorbers of fats). Each of the ladies lost from three to nine pounds the first month simply by taking a gram of calcium with each meal. Their blood chemistries also reflected significant reductions in cholesterol and triglycerides (fat). According to chemical calculations, each gram of calcium will bind 14 grams of fat! This represents a potential shunting of approximately 130 calories per meal, or 420 calories of fat per day.

A young male patient had his thyroid removed several years ago because of cancer. His parathyroid glands that regulate calcium absorption were also removed. To maintain his calcium level, he is taking six grams of calcium a day. He is so skinny he can walk through a picket fence. His cholesterol is only 128 (about half the national average), and his triglycerides only 68 (about one-quarter the national average). He eats heartily and has sedentary habits.

This concept has more importance for the prevention of fat accumulation, than for fat loss. It will not remove fat that has already accumulated. (The natural burning of fat by the body will, however, cause weight loss if burned fat is not replaced.) It will be of great benefit to the fat hyper-absorbers. Taking calcium with a diet that contains no fat will be useless. If however, you would enjoy a steak, a dressing on the salad, butter on your roll, and some ice cream for dessert, it would be prudent to take two or three 500 mg Os-Cal tablets with the meal.

The rigorous avoidance of starch and sugar is unnecessary in the prevention of fat accumulation. The body does, however, preferentially use the glucose (derived from starch and sugar) for its energy source. Eating sugar and starch protects the fat stores from being burned for energy. Hence, there is reason to limit carbohydrates if you wish to lose weight. The less carbohydrate available for energy, the more the fat reserves must be used. However, too great restriction of carbohydrates causes problems. Near complete elimination of carbohydrates, as is employed in many weight loss programs, results in *ketoacidosis*. While it is a rapid means of losing weight, it is dangerous. Incomplete burning of fats results in the formation of keto acids. These acidify the blood, reducing its oxygen–carrying capacity. Resistance to infection is greatly reduced, bone calcium is reabsorbed and excreted, and energy levels are also reduced. Ketoacidosis occurs in starvation and in uncontrolled diabetes when the individual cannot burn glucose. It can also result from a high protein or high fat diet. You need not starve to become ketotic.

Before the body begins its rapid burning of fat in ketosis, much of the protein from the muscles is burned. In order to avoid this, a weight reduction diet should contain at least a maintenance level of protein and a modest amount of carbohydrate to avoid ketosis.

General Considerations for Would–Be Dieters

Consideration #1: There is a fundamental law of physics which operates in nature. It is a law like the law of gravity, in that it cannot be broken. This law states that a small amount of heat energy transforms into a large amount of mechanical motion energy.

An illustration of this law is the burning of a gallon of gasoline. It is able to push a 4,000–pound automobile for 20 miles! Incredible is it not? Remember, this law is unbreakable. What it means to you is that, if you are trying to lose weight, a pound of fat (which is as energy–laden as gasoline) can propel your body "20 miles" or more, whether you choose to run or walk. Translated into practical terms, it means that exercise is not an efficient, easy means of losing weight. And probably not a very pleasant one either. In the first place, if you were athletically inclined and enjoyed prolonged walking or running, you would not have the weight problem you are presently concerned about. Sadly, too, walking is a very efficient expenditure of energy. You get a great many miles on that pound of fat (13 is the generally accepted mileage from a pound of fat). While it is true that you do lose weight through exercise, and the exercise is good for you in other ways, it is *not* a fast, easy way to lose weight.

What about exercise machines and appliances? They are great if they get you to exercise, but they will not bring about any rapid weight loss. Nearly all the gadgets advertised for losing weight are gimmicks and are generally useless. The 13 miles of exercise per pound of fat applies no matter how you choose to do the exercise.

Consideration #2: To maintain life, there must be a continuous expenditure of energy. The maintenance of heart beat, respiratory muscle action, digestion, muscle tone, and body heat requires a constant utilization of heat energy. This is called basal metabolism. When a person does not eat, calories of stored energy (fat and protein) are burned. (This is like tearing up the box cars for fuel to keep the locomotive running.) A second unbreakable law in nature states that if you do not eat, you must lose weight. This is the weight of the fuel used from body stores. If you wish to lose weight, all you have to do is to eat less. It has been determined that each pound of fat is equivalent to about 3,600 calories. Thus, if you burn 2,000 calories in a day, and eat 2,000 calories, you neither gain or lose. If you burn 2,000 calories a day and eat 2,600 calories, the extra 600 calories per day for a week will cause you to gain about one pound. If you burn 2,000 calories per day, and only eat 1,400 calories, the daily deficit of 600 calories will cause you to burn off a pound of fat per week. If you wish to

lose more, you must curtail eating even more (600 calories a day is the amount of food equivalent to nine slices
of bread).

The energy needs of different individuals vary
greatly. The lumberjack may require 7,000 or 8,000 calories per day to maintain a stable weight. The octoge-
narian who lies in bed most of the time may maintain
weight on as little as 800 calories a day. Generally, a
large person will expend more calories than a smaller
one. The stevedore who burns 6,000 calories a day can
eat 2,000 calories a day and still lose a pound a day,
while the 120–pound secretary who expends 1,200 calories a day, cannot lose a pound by starving in less than
three days! Practically speaking then, if you wish to lose
weight, you must sharply reduce the amount of food you
eat daily. If you reduce your food intake, your basal
metabolism will bring about a weight loss—all you have
to do is sit back and let it happen.

Consideration #3: Following are some suggestions for
reducing food intake.

Most people overeat because they are anxious, not
because they are hungry. Food is a very potent tranquil-
izer (very pleasant, too). Whether from infancy, when
the source of food was a source of comfort and security,
or from an evolutionary origin, is immaterial. The fact
is, that food is eaten most often because it has a calming
effect on the nervous system. The kind of food is less of
a factor in allaying anxiety than the bulk, the timeli-
ness, and the act of eating.

Translated into practical terms, you can satisfy this
anxiety–drive to eat just as well with foods that are low

in calories as with highly caloric ones. So have lots of low-calorie foods at hand to eat for the alleviation of anxiety. Diet soda pop is such a "food." It is filling and you think you are getting something when, in fact, you are getting only colored water. Celery sticks, radishes and carrot sticks are good ways to fulfill your need for "tranquilization" food.

In trying to cut down on your food consumption, remember: *It is easier to resist temptation on the supermarket shelf than to resist it on the refrigerator shelf.* If you would lose weight, the easiest effective action is not to bring all the goodies home from the store. Then when you feel the urge to eat, you will satisfy it with tomatoes, celery, and diet pop. There is a great difference in the caloric contents of different foods. Fats and oils have the most calories per gram or pound.

If you wish to lose weight, you must cut down sharply on fatty foods: meats, butter pastries, etc. Breads, potatoes, and cereals are fairly high in calories and we tend to eat rather large quantities of these. To lose weight, these foods must also be curbed. Fresh vegetables commonly used in salads tend to be low in calories. To satisfy your need for food and bulk, you can still lose weight by increasing the amount of these foods while decreasing the fats and carbohydrates.

Consideration #4: A day–to–day weight variation of three or four pounds is quite normal. This weight variation is due to water retention and is temporary. High intake of salt causes water to be retained; it is shed later as the salt is removed from the body by the kidneys. A surprisingly small amount of salt will cause a disturbingly large water accumulation. This water retention is of the order of nine pounds of water for one teaspoon of salt! It is very easy to gain four or five pounds after one salty meal (Note: you do not have to eat four or five pounds of food to gain five pounds).

Consideration #5: Because of the physical, chemical and health laws involved, it is unrealistic to expect very rapid weight losses by any safe means. A three-pound-per-week loss is significant, and no one should be discouraged that he or she is not losing more rapidly. Total starvation will cause weight losses of up to a pound a day, but starvation beyond a few days results in severe ketoacidosis that predisposes one to infection and other health hazards.

Consideration #6: What is a good reducing diet? One that is extremely effective and meets the body's needs for carbohydrate, protein, and vitamins has been worked out by Dr. Irwin S. Freedman of Alexandria, Virginia. This diet includes a milk–based drink in the morning to provide the protein needs of the day, and a carbohydrate pudding meal for lunch and dinner. At bedtime, a salad is eaten for fiber and bulk. This diet is built around Sustacal liquid and pudding. Sustacal is a special food supplement developed for use in hospitals and nursing homes. It is fortified with vitamins and minerals and one can remain on this low-caloric (1,000 calories) diet for prolonged periods of time without danger of malnutrition or ketoacidosis. Many other weight loss programs lack the feature of maintaining protein and avoiding ketosis that is built into this diet.

THE FREEDMAN DIET

Dr. Irwin S. Freedman's diet is a balanced, 1000–calorie plan. It is admittedly spartan. The food list is the diet. You do not take the Sustacal *with* your food—it is all the food you eat.

The morning Sustacal drink is a high protein preparation to reduce muscle protein loss that usually occurs during low-calorie diet plans. (The body prefers to burn some of its protein rather than the fat it stores.)

The Sustacal puddings and liquid are vitamin- and mineral-fortified. (They do contain corn sweetener—fructose intolerant people should beware.) It is generally very safe to follow this outline for one month. The puddings are sugar and starch based. This is important as it prevents the ketoacidosis that may accompany the fast weight loss plans, such as the Dr. Gibbons's quick weight loss plan. (Note: it too stresses protein to protect the muscle mass.)

The diet is hard to get used to, but it is one that tends to reduce the cheating that usually spoils any weight loss program.

BREAKFAST: *1 cup of coffee or tea
1 can of SUSTACAL LIQUID, 8 oz.

LUNCH: 1 diet soda
1 SUSTACAL PUDDING, 5 oz.

DINNER: *1 diet soda or cup of coffee or tea
1 can SUSTACAL PUDDING, 5 oz.

8 to 9 P.M.:   1 diet soda
1 small tossed salad, no meat or cheese, 2 tsp. normal salad dressing

NOTE: *You may use artificial sweetener,
                         but no cream or sugar.
                         **Water, diet soda, coffee, or tea
                         without sugar or cream, may be used
                         between meals.
                         ***SUSTACAL LIQUID available
                         Chocolate, Vanilla, Eggnog
                         SUSTACAL PUDDING available
                         Chocolate, Vanilla, Butterscotch
         (Reprinted with permission of Irwin S. Freedman, M.D.)

Consideration #7: A positive mental attitude is essential to motivate one to the self–denial of not eating unneeded food. Exercise is a hard way to bring about weight loss. A much easier way is to reduce food consumption, then to sit back and let the basal metabolism burn the excess energy stores (fat).

Consideration #8: Weight reduction clubs such as Weight Watchers and TOPS are helpful in motivating you to adhere to the dietary restraints needed to lose weight and keep it off.

Consideration #9: A programmed weight loss of more than 10 pounds should be undertaken only under medical supervision. Marked changes in exercise and diet may impose problems on a latent diabetic or on an individual with unrecognized anemia, heart or kidney disease. Those who are overweight because of underactive thyroid glands may starve and exercise and still lose little due to their very low basal metabolism. For them, weight control may be brought about by correcting the thyroid abnormality.

Consideration #10: What about the advertised quick ways to lose weight? The preceding principles apply whether you choose to try the grapefruit diet, the cottage cheese diet, the Cambridge diet, Weight Watchers, or others. Ads in various magazines spread claims of two pounds weight loss per day. This can be done with diet and water restriction for one or two days. It cannot be sustained; if it could, it would be dangerous.

What about diet pills—the easy quick fix? Every day millions of Americans visit their physicians and ask for diet pills with the anticipation that taking them will make them lose weight. Do they really work? They work only if they cause you to eat less. If they do not, they are useless. These drugs are powerful stimulants. They have a side effect of depressing the appetite. It is for this side effect that people take them. The drugs do not cause any weight loss directly. They may curb your appetite so you eat less. The weight loss comes only from eating less, not from the action of the pill.

Many people go to their doctors and ask for water pills to help them lose weight. Diuretics cause a rapid loss of two to four pounds—of water. They do not cause any loss of fat. The sudden weight loss tickles the vanity but, in a day or two, most of the water is replaced and the weight returns to its original value.

Consideration #11: A "short cut" diet which involves partial starvation by excluding all carbohydrates will result in a rapid weight loss by forcing the body to burn its fat. This is not a healthy diet, and it should not be used unless one is in good health and then for no longer than a month. Carbohydrates (sugars and starches) are the gasoline the body was designed to run on. Just as an auto can be forced to run on gasoline substitutes (usually very inefficiently), the body can be forced to run on fat and protein. When carbohydrates are completely denied, the body can strip the nitrogen from amino acids (the building blocks of protein). This provides a considerable source of carbohydrate to operate on for a while— but at the expense of muscle loss.

The ideal is to get rid of the fat, not the muscles. When this source of energy is depleted, the fat stores are burned.

Curiously, in this starvation situation, fat does not burn efficiently. Like burning old tires, there is more smoke than flame produced. The inefficiently burned fat forms soluble unburned intermediates which are passed in the urine and breath. (These make the peculiar breath odor that comes from extremely ill persons whose metabolism is in a state of starvation.) This situation is called ketoacidosis. With keto acids being excreted in the urine and through the lungs, there is a rapid weight loss. A person will lose about a pound a day if he is in ketoacidosis. While ketosis causes a rapid weight loss, it is not a healthy state. As noted previously, it is not recommended for anyone beyond a month at a time. A high protein intake is suggested during a ketogenic diet to protect muscle proteins as much as possible. A ketogenic, quick-weight-loss diet is listed on page 124.

Consideration #12: Recent studies have indicated that the human animal does not readily change carbohydrate into fat. This is an important principle. It means that the fats you deposit in your body come from fats you consume, not from fats made from carbohydrates.

Since the body preferentially burns carbohydrates, dietary sugar and starch prevent the burning of fat stores. There is a relationship between obesity and carbohydrate excess. Carbohydrates prevent the burning of fat. The most rapid means of losing weight is the ketogenic diet—the elimination of all carbohydrates from the diet. This forces the body to burn stored fat. The rapid weight loss diet that follows is based on this principle. On this diet, the author was able to lose five pounds of weight a week while eating a pound of Kentucky Fried Chicken a day!

The knowledge that body fat comes only from fat absorbed from the intestine allows another weight loss short cut. Fat absorption can be greatly reduced by taking calcium carbonate supplements. Calcium will combine with fat and prevent its absorption by turning it into insoluble soap. (As discussed previously, this same chemical reaction makes bathtub rings—the calcium in hard water combines with oils from the skin and soap to form the curdy substance that sticks to the sides of the tub.) Calcium supplements with meals are particularly useful in preventing the accumulation of new fat. It will not, however, cause old fat to be burned at an increased rate.

The quick weight loss diet combined with calcium supplementation forces the body to burn stored fat at a very rapid rate as fat metabolism without carbohydrates is very inefficient and wasteful. This diet is not to be used by persons who are not in otherwise good health.

DR. GIBBONS'S QUICK WEIGHT–LOSS DIET

CALCIUM CARBONATE: Take two 650 mg Os-Cal or K Mart generic calcium carbonate tablets with each meal.

LIST #1: The following may be eaten without restrictions as to amount.

Seasonings:
Salt, pepper, garlic, lemon, mint, mustard, parsley, nutmeg, vanilla, cinnamon, celery salt and vinegar

Vegetables: You may eat unrestricted amounts of the following raw. Limit cooked vegetables to one cup.

Asparagus	Lettuce
Broccoli	Mushrooms
Cabbage	Peppers (green or red)
Cauliflower	Radishes
Celery	Sauerkraut
Cucumbers	Squash
Eggplant	String beans
Greens (beet, chard, collard,	Tomatoes
kale, spinach, turnip)	Watercress

Meats: Amounts restricted to the equivalent of three hard-boiled eggs a day.
Beef, pork, fish, poultry, eggs, cheese (cheddar, swiss, cottage, etc.)

Fats: Small amounts.
Avocado, bacon, butter or margarine, dressings (French, mayonnaise, Roquefort), cooking oils and olives. (With fat–containing meals, take calcium carbonate.)

Miscellaneous: Unrestricted.

Diet pop

Coffee or tea without sugar

Non-caloric sweeteners

Bouillon

Sour or dill pickles

Artificially sweetened gelatin desserts

LIST #2: The following should be scrupulously avoided.

All foods containing sugar or starch, including all fruits (except tomatoes), all breads, cakes, crackers, cereals, milk, candy and sugar–containing soda pop, ice cream, corn, beans, potatoes and pasta.

The Calcium Paradox

Historically, kidney stone formers have been cautioned to avoid hard water, calcium supplements and dairy foods, as the calcium in them would contribute to kidney stones. Reason would suggest this to be the case. It has been feared that excess calcium would cause the formation of calcium oxalate stones. This fear presented a particular problem for women who were advised to take calcium supplements to avoid osteoporosis. Were you causing kidney stones by trying to avoid osteoporosis?

In the unit on kidney stones, it was pointed out that in irritable bowel disease, excessive calcium is absorbed from the intestine which then overloads the kidneys' excretory ability. Reason would recommend caution in putting large amounts of calcium in this leaky system that is known to allow too much of the element into the blood.

In the section on weight control, a calcium supplement of one gram per fat–bearing meal was recommended as a measure to control weight by preventing
fat absorption. Is there a hazard in taking what
amounts to very large amounts of calcium? Are calcium
supplements courting danger? Will they cause kidney
stones?

The answer is no. Paradoxically, the calcium supplements are more likely to prevent kidney stones than to
cause them because large amounts of calcium will block
its own absorption. Calcium supplements of this magni-
tude will decrease the acidity of the bowel contents. As
the acidity of the bowel decreases (even by a small in-
crement), the solubility of calcium diminishes sharply
and insoluble calcium cannot be absorbed. (You cannot
make the contents of the bowel too alkaline with calcium carbonate either, because it becomes insoluble and
inert near neutral pH.) You cannot cause excessive calcium absorportion by giving calcium carbonate (though
it may be possible with some other salts of calcium).
The best protection from excess calcium absorption is
the avoidance of food elements that ferment and produce
acid in the intestines.

Appearing in *Consult*, May 1986, was an excellent
review article by Dr. Alan G. Wasserstein, Assistant
Professor of Medicine at the University of Pennsylvania
School of Medicine. In the article, Dr. Wasserstein made
some important points:

> In the intestinal lumen, calcium and oxalate form an
> insoluble and poorly absorbed complex. When free cal-
> cium in the intestinal lumen decreases, free oxalate

increases, and so does the absorption of such oxalate. . . .
This is important: restricting dietary calcium may do
more harm than good if it results in increased urinary
oxalate excretion. A small increase in such urine oxalate excretion could enhance stone formation more
than would a large increase in urinary calcium
excretion. . . . Treat hyper-oxaluria by restricting dietary oxalate and increasing calcium intake. This
should help to prevent calcium stone formation. . . . A
calcium carbonate supplement of 1.3 grams twice a day
(which provides about 1,000 mg of elemental calcium)
usually effectively reduces urine oxalate excretion by
patients with enteric hyperoxaluria. There is little risk
of exacerbating stone formation by engendering hypercalciuria because such patients tend to absorb calcium
poorly and they excrete little of it.

Dr. Martin Lipkin of the Memorial Sloan–Kettering
Cancer Center in New York City reported findings that
calcium supplements may significantly reduce the
chances of developing cancer of the colon in irritable
bowel patients (*New England Journal of Medicine*,
313:22, 1381, 1985).

Ten patients at risk for a type of colon cancer that
tends to run in families were studied by researchers
from the Memorial Sloan–Kettering Cancer Center and
from Cornell University, New York. None of the patients had cancer, but the cells in the linings of their
colons were growing much more rapidly than normal.
This cell proliferation may be an indication of likely
cancer development. After taking 1,250 mg of calcium
a day (equal to about one-and-a-half times the recommended daily allowance for adults) in the form of cal-

cium carbonate for two to three months, colon cell growth in these patients was reduced to more normal levels. This reduction in cell proliferation may also mean a reduction in the risk of cancer for these patients.

Five Reasons for IBS Victims to Take Calcium

1. Calcium supplements reduce the acidity of the food stream in the intestines. Excess lactic acid in the irritable bowel severely irritates the bowel lining. Calcium combines with lactic acid and precipitates, making it harmless. (Calcium does not neutralize alcohol, which is equally irritating and harmful to the delicate intestinal membranes. You cannot take calcium and forget about the avoidance of fermentable sugars.)

2. Calcium supplements help to soap out excessive fat from dietary sources. This is important for weight control. People with irritable bowel disease tend to absorb fat excessively and become hopelessly obese. These individuals have great difficulty keeping unwanted fat off once they lose it.

3. Calcium supplements help to soap out excess bile acid. The supplements will materially reduce blood cholesterol by eliminating the body's greatest source of this unwanted material: reabsorbed bile acid.

4. By raising the pH (reducing the acidity), calcium supplements help to greatly reduce the absorption of unwanted metals (aluminum, lead, mercury and cadmium).

5. Calcium supplements probably reduce one's

chances for bowel cancer by reducing cellular proliferation caused by irritation of the lining membranes.

Are All Calciums Created Equal?

Many have asked if it matters what kind of calcium supplements they take. Calcium is calcium, but there *are* differences in the formulations of the different products. Many calcium supplements are sweetened with sorbitol or mannitol and are highly disturbing to the irritable bowel.

Calcium carbonate has the highest calcium content per gram of tablet. The lactate, gluconate, citrate, and phosphate compounds of calcium all have heavier components making up the non-calcium portion of the preparations. These are generally more expensive and have no advantage over calcium carbonate.

Oyster shells are a favorite source of calcium. The oyster actually purifies the calcium. It selectively puts calcium into its shell, rejecting contaminants such as lead that occur in other sources such as dolomite.

Bone meal is an easily available source of calcium, but bones tend to contain lead (from air and water contamination caused by the burning of leaded fuels by automobiles). Lead causes problems for the body because, in many instances, the body mistakes lead for calcium and incorporates it in bones and in enzymes, thus making enzymes that do not work.

Bone meal produces calcium phosphate. Phosphates cause increased work for the kidneys, and tend to carry more calcium away from the body than they provide.

Pregnant women get leg cramps from calcium deficiency after taking calcium phosphate or drinking a quart of milk a day. (Milk may rob you of more calcium than it provides! This is because of its very high phosphate content. Phosphate carries calcium with it when it is excreted.) Diuretics cause excretion of calcium as well as sodium and potassium. They too may provoke leg cramps by causing a mild calcium deficiency.

A Summary

Avoiding Offending Foods

The purpose of this book is to help those who suffer from irritable bowel disease discover which foods are responsible for irritating their particular digestive systems. Most individuals with any of the irritable bowel diseases will experience improvement by avoiding fructose, lactose, sorbitol, mannitol and wheat bran. For most, eliminating these foods will give complete relief from their symptoms. For others, this diet is not the full answer. Some have peculiar intolerances to specific foods that most others can eat with impunity. For example, many irritable bowel victims complain about lettuce. The author is unaware of the specific element in lettuce that causes symptoms. Others note worsening of their disease after eating chocolate.

The important point here is that each individual must do some detective work to determine which foods are responsible for his or her symptoms. Foods that cause gas formation, loose stools, pain or bloating are to be avoided. The first suspects to be considered are the sugars listed above and wheat bran. All humans are irritated by sorbitol and mannitol. These are to be carefully avoided by everyone with a tendency to irritable bowel disease.

Appendix A

The following subjects are only indirectly related to irritable bowel disease. They are topics frequently mentioned in letters to the Colitis Club, and are included for those to whom they may be applicable.

Restless Legs Syndrome

Several letters to the Colitis Club mentioned anxious legs. No one has linked the two conditions but the frequent mention of the problem by those with irritable bowel syndromes at least raises the suspicion of an association. A few of their letters were published and a flood of "cures" were offered (everyone loves to play doctor). These letters prompted a search of the medical literature to see what the professors had to say about the "restless legs syndrome" as it is referred to in medical writings.

Restless legs syndrome has been recognized for a long time. It was described by Thomas Willis in 1685 but, like the weather everyone talks about, restless legs is a condition no one is able to do anything about. In the January, 1986 issue of *AFP Journal*, Dr. Gary N. Fox summed up the state of our knowledge accumulated since Willis's time.

> Many pharmacologic agents have been reported to be effective in treating restless legs syndrome, although few double-blind studies of drug therapy have been recorded. No surgical or physical modalities have proved consistently beneficial." Another author remarked . . . "it can be said that nothing essentially new has been forthcoming."

Comments reported by the writers from their patients in the articles on restless legs are nightmarishly descriptive:

"It feels as if my whole leg was full of small worms."
"As if ants were running up and down my bones." "It
feels like an internal itch." "A creeping sensation." "It
is a diabolical feeling." "I would not wish it on my
worst enemy." "It is worse than any ordinary illness."

These colorful descriptions are probably due to the fact
that the miserable sensation does not resemble any
other known phenomenon that could be used for comparison. Two authors adamantly stated, "The pathogen-
esis is unknown, but the ailment is not psychogenic,"
as some have asserted. One patient probably put it best:
"Doctor, unless you have had it, you can't know what it
feels like."

These statements set off fire alarm bells ringing in
the author. I said to myself, "I am a doctor, and I do
know how it feels. I have restless legs syndrome. Perhaps I can give some insight into the nature of the beast
that non-sufferers do not know about."

Recognized as a common cause of insomnia, restless
legs most often acts up when first retiring to bed. It
causes a *hyperesthesia*, a greatly amplified sensation of
touch. The legs cannot tolerate the touching of one by
the other, the touching of bed clothes or being touched
by another person. (Paradoxically, slight touches provoke the most unpleasant sensation.) There is also an
intolerance to heat. Even in very cold environs, the victim will sleep with the feet uncovered. Complete temporary relief comes from walking about—but one cannot
get any sleep that way. Restless legs also annoy when
sitting still in meetings, movies, church, classes, and
while traveling in planes, autos and trains.

Several doctors reporting in the *Archives of Internal Medicine* tried to find some common elements that could link their 27 cases to some related cause. It was noted that the malady tended to be hereditary. Ten also had headaches, insomnia, seven had back pains, and three had irritable colon problems. The present author notes the syndrome plagued his mother, her brother and two sisters. The author and all of these relatives shared fructose intolerance–induced irritable bowel disease as well as restless legs syndrome!

The condition does tend to be hereditary. One member of a large family with several affected members seems to have discovered the cause of the malady; at least for most people. This sufferer noticed that sitting in a movie house almost invariably provoked an attack, whereas sitting in school or church did not. He was then led to conclude the candy bar he ate at the beginning of the show was the provoking element.

Following this lead, he noted that each time he had a large amount of sugar late in the day, the evening was marked with the agony of crawly legs. Other members of the family found they too could provoke the condition by eating sugar. These family members also shared irritable bowel syndrome.

Several wrote comments with their Colitis Club questionnaires that since they had been on the colitis diet and avoided lactose, fructose, sorbitol and mannitol, their burning legs have not bothered them. Perhaps we have discovered one cause of restless legs syndrome. Future surveys of the Club will seek to learn if others note improvement with the diet. Speaking for one, since following the diet, I no longer suffer from restless legs.

Hypoglycemia

Whether or not hypoglycemia is related to irritable bowel disease is unknown, but a number of colitis correspondents have written that they suffered from low blood sugar. Many complained that their doctors told them, "There is no such thing." Low blood sugar does occur, paradoxically, after eating large amounts of sugar. Much of the information circulated about hypoglycemia is not factual and current treatment tends to aggravate the condition rather than help it. Often the treatment is worse than the ailment.

Hypoglycemia, commonly referred to means low blood sugar. Sugar, specifically glucose, is the gasoline the creator designed the body machine to run on. When the blood sugar gets too low, you run like you are out of gas—weak, tired; common activities require great effort. Other symptoms may follow, such as malaise, nausea, severe headache, irritability and depression.

Oddly, the common form of hypoglycemia is related to *excess* sugar ingestion. If you believe in evolution, picture man in past ages with a diet devoid of concentrated sugars. He has not developed the facility in his body to handle sudden large surges of sugar. It has been only in the past fifty years that sugar in large amounts has been available to the general population. Over–ingestion of sugar is common in our present diets, but in the past, sugar had been a great luxury in the form of small amounts of honey.

When a person ingests a large amount of sugar, it is rapidly absorbed into the blood. Absorption begins in the mouth and continues in the stomach (other foods are not absorbed until they get into the small bowel). This rapid absorption of sugar abruptly raises the glucose level. When the blood sugar rises, the body supposes it to be an enormous meal, and calls for a correspondingly large amount of insulin to deal with it. In some persons, much more insulin is released than is actually needed for the amount of sugar present. The sugar load is rapidly turned into storage glycogen in the liver for reserve fuel. The blood sugar elevation lasts for about an hour, after which the excess insulin begins rapidly decreasing the blood sugar and suddenly, the level falls below normal and hypoglycemia is present. The activity of the insulin lasts from 2 to 12 hours. The excess insulin may maintain the blood sugar below normal for several hours.

There are conflicting forces at play. The insulin is trying to reduce the blood sugar further, and the adrenaline trying to raise it. It is like trying to drive your car with one foot on the brakes and the other on the gas.

Most of the symptoms experienced in hypoglycemia are due to the effects of the adrenaline rather than the low sugar: sweating, trembling, heart palpitation, giddiness, nervousness and anxiety. Severe or dangerous hypoglycemia is rare. Most episodes last about an hour and are unpleasant rather than dangerous. Occasionally, hypoglycemia is of severe enough degree to cause unconsciousness and possibly seizures.

If blood sugar levels are only slightly decreased, usually no symptoms are noticed. As lower levels are reached symptoms begin to appear. Normally blood sugar ranges from 70 to 100 milligrams per 100cc of

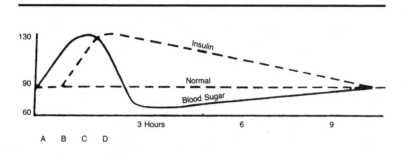

Graph 1. REACTIVE HYPOGLYCEMIA

A Sugar ingested
B Blood sugar elevation triggering insulin production
C Blood sugar drops below normal while insulin level remains high
D Continued depressed blood sugar due to continued excess insulin = Reactive Hypoglycemia

On the above chart, something else is occurring. While the blood sugar is below normal the body tries to raise the low blood sugar. It does so not by decreasing insulin, but by releasing adrenaline hormone which acts to raise blood sugar. Adrenaline works by calling up sugar from the liver glycogen store and from conversion of protein into sugar.

blood. Most people maintain a level of about 90 mg most of the time. As levels fall to the 60 mg per 100 cc level, drowsiness, laziness, and weakness are likely to be noticed. As a lower level of 50 mg is reached, more pronounced symptoms appear. Here is where adrenaline begins to be produced to prop up the falling sugar and protect vital structures such as the brain from energy deprivation. Sweating is noted, the heart beats faster and pounds. Headache is apt to occur and confusion develops as the brain gets insufficient fuel.

As the blood sugar drops further, personality changes occur. The person may become belligerent and combative, speech is garbled and as the sugar level drops a little further, coma ensues and seizures are likely as the brain now has too little sugar for its energy requirements. If the sugar drops more, brain cell damage or death is likely as glucose is the only fuel brain cells can use for energy. Depriving the brain of either oxygen or glucose for only a few minutes injures or destroys it. These extremely low blood sugar levels usually occur with accidental insulin overdosage for diabetes.

To prevent these periods of low blood sugar from happening, one must avoid large boluses of sugar that overstimulate insulin release. A breakfast of waffles or pancakes and syrup is the surest way to overload with sugar. Eating candy or drinking soda pop in place of a meal will often result in hypoglycemia. Ice cream eaten alone produces the sharp rise in blood sugar that may be followed by a sharp fall. Eating a breakfast that is mainly starch, such as cereal, is the best assurance of avoiding low blood sugar. The process of digesting starch involves its conversion into glucose in the intestine, then its absorption into the blood. Starch also stimulates insulin production but only after it has been partially changed into sugar. The process of changing the starch into sugar avoids the rapid absorption of glucose; rather the glucose is fed into the blood over a longer period of time and huge releases of insulin do not occur. The treatment of hypoglycemia consists of eating starches and avoiding large quantities of sugar.

Hypoglycemia is the condition opposite of diabetes. In diabetes, there is decreased insulin and sugar accumulates in the blood. The main part of the treatment is to reduce the amount of sugar eaten (this includes sugar which will come from converted starch). Here a low carbohydrate–high protein diet may be inappropriate. You would not treat the diabetic who has too much sugar by giving him more, neither treat the hypoglycemic who has too little sugar by giving him less. This is exactly what is most often recommended for hypoglycemia, a low carbohydrate–high protein diet. What is needed is a high starch diet, more like our ancestors ate eons ago, the diet the human body was designed for.

This graph shows the blood sugar response to starch and insulin: a slow release of sugar into the blood.

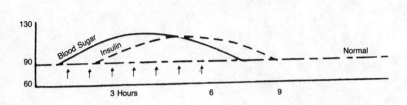

Graph 2. BLOOD SUGAR RESPONSE TO STARCH AND INSULIN

Here the insulin released matches the need of the sugar in the blood. The arrows represent sugar being released slowly into the blood over a period of time.

Of itself, starch does not stimulate insulin production. It lies inert in the intestine until it is changed to sugar by the digestive processes. When it appears in the blood as sugar, the sugar calls forth the insulin as it is needed.

Appendix B

The Absence of Cancer Among the Navaho Indians of San Juan County, Utah

The virtual absence of cancer among the Navaho Indians of Southern Utah suggests some pertinent clues relative to the cause and prevention of cancer. For the past 30 years, the physicians of San Juan County Hospital have been caring for the 5,000 Anglo and 5,000 Navaho residents of the county. During this period they were unable to find a single case of breast cancer among any of the Navaho women. Other cancers have been equally rare. All cancer cases in both populations were tabulated for a five-year period. Food vectors for animal transcriptase-producing viruses appear to be the factor that is strikingly different in the Navaho and Anglo diets.

The Prevalence of Cancer in the U.S.

Statisticians in the Government Accounting Office recently pointed out that the emperor really had no clothes on, that is, that cancer rates are actually increasing about one percent each year for most tumor types. One in three Americans are destined to develop cancer. One in nine American women will develop breast cancer, and by the year 2,000, it is estimated that 40 percent of the population will at some time develop cancer. While the national cancer incidence has been increasing—in spite of the efforts and expenditure of billions of dollars by the National Cancer Institute, the American Cancer Society and the cancer research community[1]—the Navahos have remained virtually free of the disease.

The major thrusts of the National Cancer Institute and the research communities have been to find a "cure" for cancer when they should have been working on means of prevention. Clearly, the burning need is for means of cancer prevention. The current goals to find cancer cures appear to be noble but are misdirected. (Cures for syphilis and gonorrhea are widely known, but having cures has not greatly reduced the incidence of these diseases. We have no cures for polio or smallpox, but because we have preventive measures, smallpox has been eliminated from the Earth and polio has been virtually eliminated from developed countries.)

The efforts to find cures have made some advances, but progress in treating the more common malignancies has been disappointing. According to the GAO report, the perceived improved survival rates for cancer victims over the recent years are mainly due to earlier diagnosis. This reflects an apparent improvement in survival after cancer discovery rather than any great advances in treatment. Cancer victims only appear to be living longer in a great many cases because of the earlier detection of their tumors.

Finding means of preventing cancer should be the first priority of science. Efforts to find these means have to a large extent been wasted. Over the past thirty years enormous resources have been, and still are being, expended in proving and disproving that birth control pills and saccharin may cause cancer.

The absence of cancer among the Navaho Indians of San Juan County, Utah gives me strong reason to believe that cancer can be prevented and avoided. It also suggests that the means are not complicated, and whatever factors protect these people, they operate without their having to give thought to it.

To avoid getting cancer, according to the National Cancer Institute and the American Cancer Society, you should follow a low-fat diet, eat green and yellow vegetables, increase dietary fiber and be a nonsmoker. Except for the latter, these measures have not proven very effective in preventing cancer and are recommended on the thinnest evidence.

The Paradox of the Navahos

The Navahos as a group eat a diet high in fat. A typical diet consists of mutton stew, bread deep-fried in mutton tallow, potato chips, soda pop, coffee, beer, candy and Twinkies. They eat virtually no fiber and no vegetables. The nutritional content of their diet is a disaster. Their sanitation in many instances is unbelievably bad. Many draw water from open creeks and have no sanitary facilities (not even outhouses). In spite of violating all of these health rules, they do not get cancer.

San Juan County, Utah provides a unique setting in which to study cancer among Native Americans. The population of this county consists of approximately 5,000 Navaho Indians and the same number of Anglo residents. Cancer occurrence among the Navaho population was compared with the number of cases occurring among the Anglo residents in the same period. The Anglos in the county were a "gold standard," so to speak. They too had a relatively low cancer expectancy being rural, mostly middle-class, non-smoking, non-drinking Mormons. The years 1969 through 1973 were chosen as the test period as hospital records in the region were available for this interval.

All the cases of cancer occurring in residents of San Juan County over the five-year period of 1969 through 1973 were tabulated. In gathering the data for the study, the Monument Valley Hospital operated by the Seventh-day Adventist Church was the first to be audited. The hospital had begun operation in 1960. In thirteen years of operation, the hospital had admitted 13,000 patients. These were almost exclusively Navaho Indians. Of these, only thirteen had been found to have had cancer. In the five-year test period, the rate had been constant. They had treated five patients with cancer. One of their early cases had been a Navaho woman with breast cancer. They could give no details on her life style, whether it had been according to Navaho tradition or not. (This small hospital treats mostly Arizona residents which may have made the San Juan Indian number erroneously high.) No one had studied the striking rarity of cancer among their patients before.

The San Juan Hospital in Monticello, Utah is a small rural hospital that serves all the residents of the county. The patient breakdown was sixty percent Anglo and forty percent Indian in the test period. During this five-year period, the San Juan Hospital had 8,522 admissions and had treated 97 patients for cancer. Only three of these cancer victims had been Navaho. One had bone cancer, one ovarian, and one cancer of the prostate. Among the Anglos seven had breast cancer, eight had prostate cancers, six colon cancers occurred, eight lung cancers, twenty-one skin, eight uterine, fifteen of the cervix, and twenty-two cases of cancer were in other sites.

My records in the Blanding clinic (the author's office), revealed nine Anglos and one Native American had been treated for malignancies during the test period.

The medical record clerks at the Southwest Memorial Hospital in Cortez, Colorado searched their files to identify San Juan County residents they had treated for cancer. They found four individuals, all Indian. They had treated one gall bladder carcinoma, one colon, a lymphoma and one prostatic cancer. This case of prostatic cancer was the same man treated for this disease in the San Juan Hospital.

Amazingly, this was the only case of prostate cancer

in a San Juan County Navaho ever documented. He was an old, very traditional Navaho who lived far out in the desert in a mud hut "hogan." He was the Indians' Indian. Whatever protects Navahos from cancer should have protected this man. He had been operated on in Southwest Memorial Hospital for prostate cancer. I had treated this individual and his wife in the San Juan Hospital on several occasions. A social worker suggested an association that could possibly explain why this individual should be the sole victim of this malignancy: "I know him," he said. "He is the old man with only one eye. He lives right next to Hatch's Trading Post. He is the old man that has chickens." (Traditionally, Navahos avoid birds. To them flight is possibly only by magic, and magic is to be religiously avoided.) It appeared significant to me that this man had chickens. The only Navaho to get prostate cancer happened also to be the only Navaho in the county who raised chickens and ate eggs.

Next surveyed was the United States Public Health Service Hospital at Shiprock, New Mexico. The record keepers provided the charts of Utah Navahos they had treated for cancer. There were only five patients. One of these had both skin and stomach cancer. They had also seen a leukemia, a cervical and a thyroid cancer. They commented that cancer has been a very rare disease at this hospital that treats only Native American patients.

The Montezuma Creek Clinic in Montezuma Creek, Utah provides service for a large portion of the San Juan County Indian population. Dr. Dean Benedict, M.D., its Medical Director, reported that a bowel tumor

had been the only cancer he had seen in the eight years
he had operated the clinic, which averaged thirty patients a day.

To complete the survey, the discovered cases from
the hospitals and clinics were compared to and supple-
mented with the records of the Utah State Tumor Regis-
try in Salt Lake City. (Some cancer patients either left
the rural area for treatment, or were referred to the
medical centers upstate by the local doctors.) With the
cases furnished by this facility, all the cancers occurring
in the residents of San Juan County for the study period
were documented.

What the Study Showed

The survey showed that cancer occurrence among the
Navaho residents of San Juan County was indeed very
rare. Most striking was the absence among the Navahos
of those cancers most common among their Anglo neighbors and the American population as a whole. Conspicuously absent were breast and lung cancers. Nearly as
rare were malignancies of the skin, cervix, uterus and
colon. The following is the tally of all of the cancers in
Navahos of San Juan County, Utah during the years
1969 through 1973:

	Anglos	Navahos
Breast cancer	14	0
Prostate cancer	18	1
Cervical cancer	15	2
Skin cancer	23	2

	Anglos	Navahos
Uterine cancer	12	1
Lung cancer	13	0
Colon cancer	11	1
Pancreatic cancer	6	2
Stomach cancer	1	2
Gall bladder	0	3
Other	43	6
Total cancer occurrence	156	20

What factors could account for this great disparity? Did the Anglos get better care and more accurate diagnoses? In the San Juan and Southwest Memorial Hospitals, and in the Blanding Clinic, the same doctors and nurses treated both Indian and Anglo patients. There was the same high quality care given to both groups. The Navahos treated in the other facilities also received excellent care.

Could it be that the Native Americans did not avail themselves of medical care and died at home? No. Since most of their care was free, they utilized health services more frequently than the Anglos. Could hygiene be a factor? If it was, the Anglos should have come out way ahead. Most of the Navahos did not have running water, indoor plumbing or outhouses. Could it be that one group was more promiscuous than the other? It would be easy to dismiss the marked differences by saying they were due to heredity. There were other factors, however, that logically could account for the Indians not getting cancer.

Dietary habits of the Navahos contrasted sharply with those of their Anglo neighbors in three significant characteristics. These stand out as probable factors explaining the absence of cancer among the San Juan Na-

vahos. The Indians ignorantly obey these health rules
that most non-Indians ignorantly disobey:

1. Indians do not eat raw or rare meat. They thoroughly cook their meat by boiling it.

Approximately 20 percent of the cattle in our country are infected with bovine leukemia virus, an organism closely related to the HIV agent that causes AIDS.
Eating uncooked meat places one in risk of eating these viruses that cause cancer in cattle and have been demonstrated to be capable of infecting and causing cancer in sheep and chimpanzees.[2]

2. The Indians did not drink milk, either because it has been unavailable to them until recently, or because most Indian adults are lactose intolerant.

The pooling of milk from thousands of cows insures the contamination of commercial milk by the bovine leukemia and udder wart viruses. Both have been shown to be oncogenic.[3] Meischke[4] showed that pasteurization does not kill the wart virus and one must presume the leukemia virus is not eradicated either.
(The sheep and chimpanzees mentioned were given raw milk from cows that were known to be infected with this virus. In these studies, all of the test animals developed cancer.)[5]

3. Traditional Navahos do not eat eggs or birds (at least not until Col. Sanders' Kentucky Fried came to the towns surrounding the reservation).

Eggs are highly suspect as a cause of cancer because they are contaminated with several fowl leukosis viruses. The fowl leukosis viruses belong to the retrovirus family that includes the bovine leukemia, feline leukemia and the human HIV. These are communicable from chicken to chicken and are known to cause cancer in the chickens. These viruses are found in eggs. Eating raw or uncooked eggs permits the ingestion of live viruses that cause cancer—at least in the chickens. Raw or soft-cooked eggs may be included in many foods such as egg nog, salad dressings, and ice cream. A means of "pasteurizing" eggs is desperately needed—or at least the public should be cautioned to cook them well. (Heat insufficient to harden an egg is not sufficient to kill leukosis viruses.)[6]

The study strongly suggests the need for a broad education program to teach the public to only eat animal source foods that have been thoroughly cooked, or to presterilize these foods before they come to the consumer. Ideally, milk, meat and eggs would be sterilized by radiation to destroy all of the oncogenic viruses known to be present in these foods.

In Summation

The more common cancer types were found to be notably absent among the Navaho Indians of San Juan County, Utah. A comparison of cancer occurrence was made between the 5,000 Navaho and 5,000 Anglo residents of this county. I postulate that dietary non-use of eggs, milk and rare meat accounts for this difference. These same foods are known to contain reverse transcriptase viruses that are responsible for neoplasm development in the respective animals.

REFERENCES:

1. Bailar, John C. III, Smith, Elaine M., "Progress Against Cancer." *The New England Journal of Medicine* Vol. 314 No. 19. May 8, 1986.

2. McClure, H.M., Keeling, M.E., Custer, R.P., et al. "Erythroleukemia in Two Infant Chimpanzees Fed Milk from Cows Naturally Infected with the Bovine C-Type Virus." *Cancer Research* 34:2745-2757, 1974.

3. Kenyon, S.J., Ferrer, J.F., McFeeley, R.A., et al. "Induction of Lymphosarcoma in Sheep by Bovine Leukemia Virus." *Journal of the National Cancer Institute* 67:1157-1163, 1981.

4. Olson, C., Miller, L.D., et al. "Transmission of Lymphosarcoma from Cattle to Sheep. *Journal of the National Cancer Institute.* 49:1463-1467, 1972.

5. Lancaster, Wayne D., Carl Olson and William Meinke. "Quantitation of Bovine Papilloma Viral DNA in Viral-Induced Tumors." *Journal of Virology* 17:824-831, 1976.

6. Meischke, H.R.C. "In Vitro Transformation by Bovine Papilloma Virus." *Journal of Virology* 43:473-487.

SUGGESTED READINGS:

Jarrett, W.F.H., Murphy, J. & O'Neill, B.W. 1978. "Virus-induced papillomas of the alimentary tract of cattle." *International Journal of Cancer* (in press).

Miller, L.D., Miller, J.M., and Olson, C. "Innoculation of Calves with Particles Resembling C-type Virus from

Cultures of Bovine Lymphosarcoma." *Journal of the National Cancer Institute* 48:423-428, 1972.

Black, P.H., Hartley, J.W., Rowe, W. P., and Huebner, R. 1963. "Transformation of bovine tissue culture cells by bovine papilloma virus." *Nature* (London) 199:1016-1018.

Kidd, J.G., Beard, J.W., and Rous, P. 1936. "Serological reactions with a virus causing rabbit papillomas which become cancerous." I. Tests of the blood of animals carrying the papilloma. *J. Exp. Med.* 64:63-77.

Boiron, M., Levy, J.P,. Thomas, M., Friedman, J.C., and Bernard, J. 1964. "Some properties of the bovine papilloma virus." *Nature* (London) 201:423-424.

Cheville, N.F. 1966. "Studies on connective tissue tumors in the hamster produced by bovine papilloma virus." *Cancer Res.* 26:2334-2339.

Olson, C., and Cook, R. H., 1951. "Cutaneous sarcoma-like lesions of the horse caused by the agent of bovine papilloma." *Proc. Soc. Exp. Biol. Med.* 77:281-284.

Rous, P. "Transmission of a malignant new growth by means of a cell-free filtrate." *JAMA* 56:198, 1911.

Gross, Ludwik, M.D. "The Role of Viruses in Cancer, Leukemia, and Malignant Lymphomas." *Medical Times*, September 1985, pp 67-77.

ABOUT THE AUTHOR

De Lamar Gibbons, M.D., former director of research at the *Saturday Evening Post*, discovered that his own irritable bowel problems were caused by fructose. Then he discovered that hospital patients fed a lactose- and fructose-free diet saw remarkable improvement in their inflammatory bowel conditions.

Dr. Gibbons developed a questionnaire which was published in the *Saturday Evening Post*. From the tremendous response he received, he then did a study on approximately 3,000 of the respondents who followed his suggested diet, also published in the *Post*.

He discovered that patients who had arthritis along with an irritable bowel found their arthritis improved as well! Since then, Dr. Gibbons believes that the introduction of corn syrup to our daily diet in so many foodstuffs is one of the main causes of irritable bowel syndrome today. His diet, included in this book, excludes: fructose, mannitol, wheat bran, lactose, sorbitol, chili powders and spices.

Dr. Gibbons and thousands of readers of the *Saturday Evening Post* have found relief from the agony of irritable bowel syndrome—now you can too!